TRUE CRIME STORIES OF THE SOUTH CAROLINA MIDLANDS

TRUE CRIME STORIES OF THE SOUTH CAROLINA MIDLANDS

Cathy Pickens

Published by The History Press
Charleston, SC
www.historypress.com

Copyright © 2024 by Cathy Pickens LLC
All rights reserved

First published 2024

Manufactured in the United States

ISBN 9781467154468

Library of Congress Control Number: 2023945824

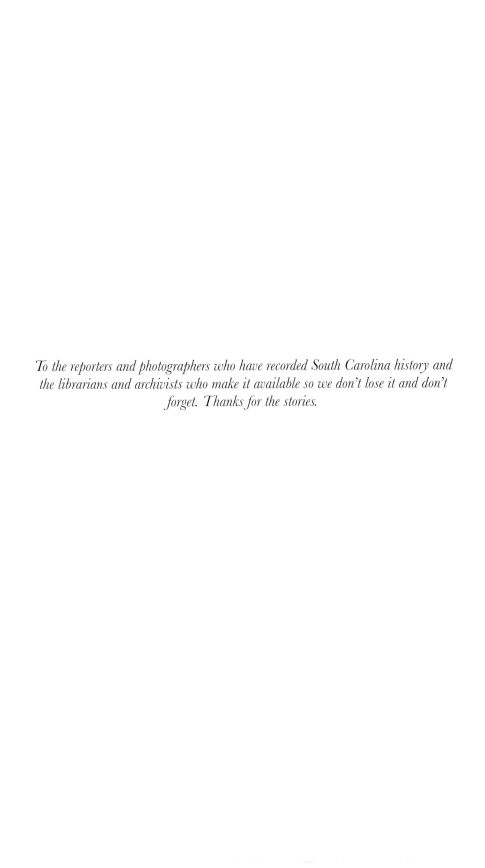

To the reporters and photographers who have recorded South Carolina history and the librarians and archivists who make it available so we don't lose it and don't forget. Thanks for the stories.

CONTENTS

Acknowledgements   9

Welcome   13

1. THE NEW FORENSICS

Suicide or Murder?   19

The Sumter Does   24

California Cop Killer   29

2. THE MISSING (AND FOUND)

The Shaw Creek Killer   33

Snatched from Her Bed   41

The Survivor Who Thrived   44

3. THE LADY KILLERS

Beatrice Snipes   47

Rose Stinnette   52

Jennie May Walker Burleson   57

4. THE POISONERS

A Short History of Poison   62

Lieutenant Samuel Epes   64

A Modern Arsenic Poisoning   67

CONTENTS

5. HEADLINE CRIMES

Pee Wee Gaskins 73
Home Alone 78
A Terrifying Summer 83

6. THE GAMBLERS

"I'm Going to Disney World!" 87
Gambling Debts and Death 92

7. THE TRICKSTERS

Terror Close to Home 97
Insurance Fraud 104
The Minister and the Hitman 106
Fire at the Farm 107

8. POLITICAL SCANDALS

Lost Trust 111
Abscam 113

9 THE LEGISLATIVE DAUGHTERS

Did He? Or Didn't He? 119
A Family Divided 126

10. SIDE TRIPS, CRIME BITS AND ODDITIES

Vicious Politics 130
Professor Greener 133
Cop Killer, Escapee and TV Fugitive 133
Columbia's Cat Burglar 136
Alimony and Murder 138

References 141
About the Author 155

ACKNOWLEDGEMENTS

MANY THANKS TO:

Friend and professional photographer Andy Hunter. For traditional and drone photography, contact andyhunterphotos@gmail.com.

Jennifer Moss, assistant curator/education specialist, Oconee History Museum, Walhalla, South Carolina, for telling me the startling story of Hoyt Hayes and sharing her extensive research file.

Margaret Dunlap and the Richland Library's Local History collection—pictures *do* tell the story.

Taylor Grooms, whose legal research provided an important puzzle piece.

Paula Connolly and her good humor, constant friendship and storyteller's eye.

Stuart Ferguson and Shakespeare & Co. Books in Highlands, North Carolina, for a quiet place to work surrounded by books and friends.

Keith Vincent and his historic courthouse postcard site (www.courthousehistory.com) with "at least one postcard from every county (or parish) in the country."

Chad Rhoad, Abigail Fleming, Jonny Foster and the mighty crew at The History Press who create such beautiful books.

As always, to Bob, who is along for every adventure.

Map of Columbia and Midlands region.

WELCOME

In its formative years, what became North Carolina and South Carolina started as a land grant that ran from the Atlantic Ocean all the way to the Pacific, presented by King Charles II of England to eight Lords Proprietor, the friends who had helped him become king. The Midlands of South Carolina was settled later than the coastal area around Charleston, and in 1786, the seat of state government moved from Charleston to Columbia and its current more central location to better serve the inland expansion of settlers.

Almost eighty years later, Sherman took such umbrage with South Carolina and its role in starting the Civil War that he set fire to its capital city, Columbia—or did he? Southerners and federals have argued about that since 1865. No one disputes that after his destructive March to the Sea in Georgia, Sherman's forces turned toward South Carolina. His troops camped across the Congaree River (roughly where the Gervais Street bridge crosses today) and lobbed shells at the unoccupied statehouse. Its construction began in the 1850s but was not complete when the war broke out. Today, brass stars mark the spots where six balls struck the granite walls on the western side. Four others struck inside the unfinished building.

But disputes still circle around whether the federal troops set the fires or whether evacuating residents or Confederate soldiers did. According to History.com, Union general Henry Slocum said, "A drunken soldier with a musket in one hand and a match in the other is not a pleasant visitor to have about the house on a dark, windy night." Sherman himself, looking back

Bronze star and damaged stonework on South Carolina State House from shelling by General Sherman's troops during the Civil War. *Courtesy of Brandon Davis via Wikimedia Commons.*

After fire destroyed Columbia in February 1865, George N. Barnard photographed the damage to the unfinished South Carolina State House. *Courtesy of the Library of Congress.*

on the events, said, "Though I never ordered it and never wished it, I have never shed any tears over the event, because I believe that it hastened what we all fought for, the end of the War." Two-thirds of the city burned on the night of February 17, 1865.

Columbia sits at the center of a state that is remarkably diverse considering its small size. The culture and foodways, the types of crops grown and the level of economic prosperity vary greatly from the coastal areas to the Backcountry or Upstate. Columbia and the surrounding Midlands sit right in the middle, at the point where settlers found rivers less navigable and farms became smaller. Where exactly are the regional lines drawn? South Carolinians like to debate everything—from barbecue (tomato, mustard or vinegar based?) to rice (Lowcountry) versus potatoes (Upstate). So naturally they debate their boundaries and dividing lines.

James L. Petrigru, a Charleston lawyer who openly opposed South Carolina's vote to secede from the Union, famously said, "South Carolina is too small for a republic and too large for an insane asylum." Columbia, home of the state's legislature, its governor's mansion and supreme court, is the stalwart center of this fractious state, between its coast—with history-rich Charleston and Beaufort and the vacation meccas of the

Photographer George N. Barnard captured the damage to Columbia viewed from the steps of the statehouse. *Courtesy of the National Archives and Records Administration via Wikimedia Commons.*

Grand Strand—and its business-focused Upstate. The region has its share of unusual crime stories. In this book, we'll explore the crimes that have helped define Columbia and this central region, ranging from Sumter to the Georgia border.

Some of those stories originate in other parts of the state but had their effect on Columbia. As one example, Pee Wee Gaskins, among the nation's most unusual serial killers, hailed from the state's Pee Dee region. His eight convictions—fewer than his fifteen confirmed murders or the one hundred he claimed he committed—sent him to Central Prison in downtown Columbia, where he cemented his sneaky, violent reputation after he was locked inside. Other stories include the murders of two state legislators' daughters twenty years apart, the suffragist who shot her rival in a Columbia restaurant, the female root doctor sent to the electric chair, the double murders that brought to light a gambling ring, cold cases solved by cutting-edge forensics and a cat burglar/psychiatrist. These stories and others helped shape the uniqueness of Columbia and the Midlands.

My family has been in the Carolinas for more than three hundred years. Because any telling naturally depends on the storyteller's choices, these are cases that, for one reason and another, captured my imagination.

View of statehouse from Columbia's Main Street before 1910. *Originally published by Southern Post Card Co., Asheville, North Carolina, via Wikimedia Commons.*

This book is not a work of investigative journalism. The information is drawn solely from published or broadcast resources—newspapers, television documentaries, podcasts, books, scholarly papers, print and online magazine articles. One of the drawbacks in recounting historical events is that accounts vary. Some reported "facts" aren't accurate, or they're at odds with someone else's memory or perception of the event. While I have worked to dig out as many points of view as I could find, I'm sure there are mistakes. My apologies in advance.

For me, what fascinates is not random violence but rather people, their lives and their relationships. Some of these stories could have happened anywhere. Some made huge headlines far away from South Carolina. Others remain writ large mostly in the hearts of the family and friends involved.

The stories, woven together, demonstrate the rich variety of those who call this part of the state home. People and their pasts matter here. The stories are worth remembering, even when they involve loss and especially when they are tempered with affection and fond memories.

Welcome to the crime stories of Columbia and the Midlands.

1

THE NEW FORENSICS

Suicide or Murder?

Time passes, lives move on, new stories fill the headlines. Those involved in difficult or tragic stories want to leave the pain in the past and thus their stories fade from memory. But often, because of the time that has elapsed, because of changes in technology and because similar questions arise in future cases, some stories continue to provide interesting points to ponder. The story of Hoyt Hayes is such a case. The hundred-year-old tale offers perspectives on the power of forensic science, but it might have disappeared without the work of Jennifer Moss at the Oconee History Museum.

In 1906, Hoyt Hayes sat in South Carolina's Central Prison in Columbia, convicted of murdering his wife. The jury couldn't reach a decision in his first trial. In his second, he was sentenced to death. On one hand, he likely felt fortunate that, days before his scheduled hanging in 1904, Governor Duncan Clinch Heyward had seen fit to commute his death penalty to a life sentence. On the other hand, Hoyt likely felt ill-used because he'd consistently and continually insisted that he hadn't shot his wife. Now, his fate rested on some handwritten letters and some handwriting experts.

In the early hours of Sunday, April 26, 1903, Lula Hayes told her husband, Hoyt, she'd heard something out in the barn. He went to investigate but found nothing out of the ordinary. While there, he fed the mule they planned to use

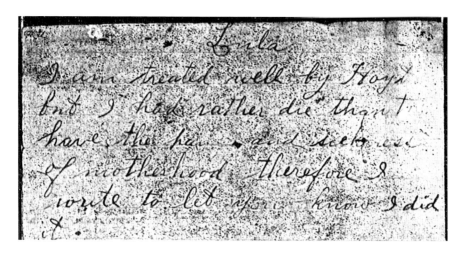

later in the day for a Sunday visit with family. He heard a muffled noise and ran to the house to find twenty-one-year-old Lula dead in the bed, "her head shot away" and a shotgun and a fireplace poker lying on the bed beside her.

Hoyt summoned his brother and a neighbor to the house as soon as he discovered the tragedy. When the men settled in the sitting room to await officials, a paperback book slipped from the seat of one of the chairs and a note fell out.

The handwritten note wasn't signed but was headed with Lula's name, almost like a casual calling card (see above).

The note read:

> *I am treated well by Hoyt*
> *but I had rather die than to*
> *have the pain and sickness*
> *of motherhood, therefore I*
> *write to let you know I did*
> *it.*

The coroner ruled her death a suicide, and she was buried. Both families were prominent in their Oconee County community. Lula's father, certain his daughter hadn't killed herself, was able to stir up suspicion about the scene in the bedroom. Though no motive for murder was shown, a coroner's jury "failed to attach blame to any person" and Hoyt "stoutly maintained his innocence," he was nonetheless arrested on May 6, on a warrant sworn out by Lula's father.

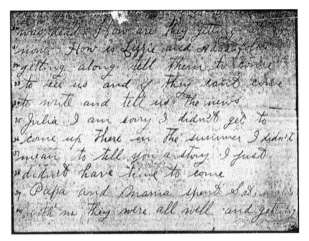

Opposite: The local newspaper reprinted the apparent suicide note handwritten by Lula Hoyt. *Courtesy of* Keowee Courier, *July 4, 1906.*

Left: As part of the trial coverage, the newspaper reprinted one of Lula Hoyt's writing samples examined by experts. *Courtesy of* Keowee Courier, *July 4, 1906.*

On November 18, 1903, after a five-day trial, a local jury found Hoyt guilty of murder.

Seven months later, the state supreme court affirmed the trial court's decision: "On the night of the tragedy, only the defendant and his wife were in the house....A gun with the load discharged and a fire poker were lying on the bed near the dead body....The prosecution submitted to the jury that from the position of the body and of the gun, and from the direction of the shot, it was impossible that Mrs. Hayes fired the gun."

An appellate court can only deal with questions of law, not fact. The state supreme court held that questions about who wrote the note and how the shot was fired were questions of fact and left for the jury to decide. The court upheld the conviction.

The governor opted to begin his own study of the case. He didn't find evidence to merit the death penalty, and in October 1904, he commuted Hoyt's sentence to life. Naturally, that decision drew comment and criticism. Some applauded Governor Heyward's decision. Some called for his resignation. One editorial summed the debate up succinctly: "In our opinion he should have been hanged, or acquitted, for he is either a black hearted murderer or an innocent man." To that writer, a life sentence left Hoyt painfully 'twixt and 'tween—neither innocent nor suitably punished, depending on the truth.

After more than a year of study and after consultation with a renowned handwriting expert, the governor agreed with the editorial writer. Heyward was convinced the evidence didn't support Hoyt's guilt, and he ordered him set free.

South Carolina Governor's Mansion where Governor Duncan Clinch Heyward resided in 1904. *Courtesy of Columbia Cigar & Tobacco Co. and the Boston Public Library, Print Department.*

That move was a political risk. Politicians are rightly reluctant to step into judicial quagmires, and letting a convicted man walk free could make the governor look soft on crime. He'd received petitions from both sides: one thousand signatures asking that Hoyt be reprieved, five hundred telling the governor to let him hang. The newspaper reported one citizen's extremist view: "On account of the prevalence of lawlessness in the State one writer had urged him [the governor] to let the accused be hanged even if he were not guilty."

But Governor Heyward made it clear he was acting on his own initiative, based on his own research and from his own belief in Hoyt's innocence. When he initially commuted the death sentence, he did so to allow time to evaluate the case further. The governor could have passed the case to the recently created state pardon board, but he said, "It would not be fair either to the board or to myself to appear now to shift the burden of responsibility from my shoulders to the shoulders of the board," since he'd already undertaken the review of the case. He'd read the court documents, reviewed the transcript of the trial testimony and studied the exhibits presented to the jury.

And he consulted David Carvalho, a "celebrated" handwriting expert employed by the district attorney in New York City, one of several experts who examined the Hayes note and certainly the most famous. In one of

Carvalho's almost nine hundred trials—a trial that for some observers confirmed his reputation as a "notorious self-promoter and headline grabber"—he crossed courthouse lines from the prosecution side to testify for the defense in the retrial of an infamous New York poisoner.

In that 1898 New York case, Harry Cornish received in the post a blue bottle of powder with a Bromo Seltzer label sitting inside a silver toothpick holder and elegantly wrapped in a Tiffany's box. Cornish thought it was a joke since he never indulged in alcohol and had no need for a hangover cure. But it was just the thing to alleviate his landlady's terrible headache—permanently. Unfortunately, the blue bottle contained mercury of cyanide, not Bromo Seltzer. The poison was apparently sent to rid a fellow Knickerbocker Club member of the irksome presence of Cornish.

Roland Molineux and Cornish were at odds because Cornish too often won in their petty disputes and athletic matches at the club and even in courting a certain woman's affections. Witnesses saw Molineux buy the silver holder. Experts said his handwriting and his odd spelling of "fourty" matched the package of poison. Molineux was convicted.

But after a second appeal in 1902, a second jury heard new testimony—this time, from David Carvalho, who said Molineux had not written the note. After deliberating only thirteen minutes, the second jury acquitted him. In *Memoirs of a Murder Man* (1930), New York detective Arthur Carey blamed missing witnesses whose testimony the second jury didn't hear as the reason for the acquittal; he never mentioned Carvalho's testimony.

Nonetheless, thanks to the Molineux case, Carvalho's reputation as a handwriting expert preceded him to South Carolina, though he wasn't the only handwriting expert involved. Others had previously testified for the defense at Hoyt's murder trial; another expert studied the note at the request of the prosecutor. Carvalho reviewed the samples for the governor. All the experts were charged with answering the key questions: "Was it written by Lula Hayes just before taking her own life, or was it written by Hoyt Hayes, a wife murderer, to save himself from the gallows?"

In his written opinion to the governor, Carvalho emphasized his "weary and painstaking study" of the samples from both Hoyt and Lula, comparing them to the questioned note. He warned how easy it was to jump to conclusions: "An experience of nearly thirty years permits me to observe how prone we all are to be affected by a corresponding likeness to be found as between correctly made single letters." So that readers could judge for themselves, the local newspaper reprinted Carvalho's detailed report in which he outlined his study of the tilt of letters and slant of lines, how letters were linked, the pressure applied to the pen, the casualness or ease of the writing and the writing styles of Lula and Hoyt.

Carvalho, along with every expert who examined the note—for the prosecution, for the defense and for the governor's independent review—all came to the same conclusion. Lula Hayes had written her suicide note.

Over one hundred years later, forensic evidence was more common but wasn't unquestioningly accepted by courts. In 2009, following several devastating revelations about lack of rigor or outright manipulation of evidence by state and federal forensics labs, a National Research Council report called for more peer-reviewed study of procedures, particularly in three areas: bite marks, hair and handwriting. A 2022 response to that call for more rigorous evaluation reported, not surprisingly, that handwriting analysis depended on whether the examiners were well-trained and experienced; inexperienced or less well-trained examiners were not as accurate.

Whether Carvalho would have passed the tests given modern-day forensic document examiners isn't known. But the prosecution and defense experts agreed that Lula had written the note. Those who knew Hoyt and Lula Hayes—apart from her father—didn't believe Hoyt killed her. The governor's pardon seemed right and proper.

On June 27, 1906, the *Keowee Courier* reported from Columbia: "About the happiest man in Columbia to-day is Hoyt Hayes, who, after being under the sentence of death, will to-morrow morning go forth from prison a free man."

The Sumter Does

When a family member or friend disappears, it sometimes marks a tragic but almost inevitable outcome for a life lost in drugs or a dangerous lifestyle. Often, though, the disappearance is completely unexpected. In either situation, a search that drags on for years is heartbreaking and exhausting, full of both hope and fear.

According to Department of Justice statistics, 600,000 people are reported missing each year in the United States. Some want to be missing—but 4,400 unidentified bodies are found each year, and 1,000 are still without names after a year.

Every state has cold case files recording bodies without names. Some died of natural causes. Some died by violence. Law enforcement follows the leads it has, but too often those leads trickle to an end and files begin gathering dust. However, the explosive growth over the last few decades of the power and reach of online searches and the diligence of amateur sleuths have connected some of those missing persons and those nameless bodies, bringing answers to some families and friends—and to the authorities and the citizen sleuths who longed to bring closure.

In South Carolina, the Sumter Does were one of the state's most puzzling unidentified bodies cases. Several elements made the case stand out. For starters, investigators had two bodies, not one—apparently the only case in the country with two murdered, unidentified victims. They were young, healthy, well cared for and apparently well-traveled. No signs of drugs or alcohol in their systems. They carried items that should have helped identify them or find where they came from—but didn't.

And their mystery remained unsolved for forty-four years.

What did investigators initially deduce about them? Where did that lead? How did those deductions match up with the reality of the young couple's lives?

The mystery started on August 9, 1976, when the two, thought to be in their late teens or early twenties, were found shot to death in Sumter County on a dirt frontage road between Interstate 95 and SC Highway 341. A truck driver who pulled off the road to take a break found them. They'd been executed, with shots to the throat, chest and back from either a .38 or .357 handgun. They had no money or identification on them.

Both were slender and casually but neatly dressed. One of the first things noted was the quality of their dental work. In 1976, long before DNA or national fingerprint databases, dental records were often the best hope for identification. The young man in particular had thousands of dollars of reconstructive work—root canals, bridge work, caps—and the work was not yet completed. The American Dental Association circulated dental X-rays to alert its members; no one responded as recognizing either victim as a patient.

Both wore nice jewelry; he had a Bulova watch and a gold and sapphire ring; she had silver rings with colored stones like jewelry made in the Southwest or Mexico. From her jewelry and a book of matches in his pocket, authorities thought they had come from or traveled through the Southwest, Nebraska or Idaho. No vehicle was found. Had they been hitchhiking, or had they been carjacked?

The autopsy showed they'd eaten fruit or ice cream with fruit in it shortly before they died. A witness thought they'd visited a farm stand off the

Florence Highway—but couldn't remember if they were traveling with anyone else or if they were driving a car.

Authorities at first wondered if they might be brother and sister, but later DNA testing disproved that. The search cast a wide net: from Nebraska, where the man might have had a car worked on, to Florida, because he was wearing a T-shirt sold only at a race in Sebring. They tried to trace the Bulova watch using its serial number; they checked with Interpol, U.S. Customs and South American contacts. No leads surfaced.

For the following year, the bodies were kept in sealed glass-topped caskets at a Sumter funeral home, waiting for someone to identify them. Through the efforts of Sheriff Ira Parnell, they were eventually interred at his church's cemetery in Oswego. Their headstones identified them as "Male—Unknown" and "Female—Unknown" and noted that "a Christian burial was given by Bethel Church August 14, 1977." Years later, Sheriff Parnell's daughter told WIS News that her father "had a tender heart" and worked for years to solve the case, unsuccessfully.

Early in the investigation, Sumter County's deputy coroner Verna Moore told AP News, "These kids belong to someone. Somewhere, somebody has got to be concerned about their whereabouts and their safety."

As the years passed, theories about the Sumter Does grew in complexity and drama. Researcher Matthew McDaniel summarized the possibilities explored: the couple had gotten crosswise with drug smugglers or organized crime (suspected because a large drug ring associated with IMSA racing made headlines in the 1980s and Jock Doe, as he was called, wore a commemorative shirt from the Sebring 1975 IMSA race); they got embroiled in the convoluted political corruption in the Sumter region at the time; they were in the federal witness protection program or running from political violence in Chile or Argentina.

Three months after the bodies were discovered—though they still weren't identified—investigators found the gun that killed them. A Wadesboro, North Carolina truck driver had the gun when he was arrested for drunk driving. The serial number was scratched off, but ballistics tests linked it to the August shootings in Sumter. The truck driver said his brother gave him the gun, which turned out to have been stolen in North Carolina's Raleigh-Durham area. The route it traveled to that dirt road off Interstate 95 and how many people had possession of it and whether the truck driver or his brother were involved in the murders couldn't be established. The gun became the only promising lead made public, though it ultimately didn't lead to an arrest.

In 2007, a couple of years before Verna Moore retired from thirty years as county coroner, she had the two bodies exhumed to get DNA samples. Verna died in 2017 at age ninety-one, two years before the DNA samples finally yielded results.

As often happens when theories develop from the thinnest of threads, none of those early investigative leads held up. By 2019, Matthew McDaniel had become curious and immersed himself in the case for about a year. The Clemson University civil engineering graduate followed old hints and tried to find answers. He did more than speculate—he funneled information to the Sumter Sheriff's Office and the county coroner, whom he thanked online for being receptive; he created a website (sumtermysterycouple.com) to keep public attention on the case, he suggested their DNA be entered in NamUs (National Missing and Unidentified System); and he encouraged the sheriff's office to pursue the latest much-publicized crime-solving tool, genetic genealogy.

The sheriff's office contacted the DNA Doe Project, which used GEDmatch and Family Tree DNA sites, the two genealogical databases that allow access for criminal investigations. As soon as the victims' DNA files were uploaded, DNA Doe Project volunteers set to work.

A quick outline of the magic of genetic genealogy doesn't do justice to all the meticulous and time-consuming work and all the individuals involved behind the scenes. On its webpage, the DNA Doe Project thanked a long list of those who helped with this case: its donors (who paid for the lab work needed); Sumter County Sheriff's Office and Investigator Charles Bonner; citizen-sleuth "Matt McDaniel for his unwavering interest in seeing the case solved"; "the National Center for Missing & Exploited Children; DNA Solutions in Oklahoma City and Astrea Forensics in Santa Cruz, California for extraction; HudsonAlpha Discovery for sequencing; Kevin Lord of Saber Investigations; GEDmatch and Family Tree DNA for providing their databases; and DDP's [DNA Doe Project] dedicated teams of volunteer genealogists." It took a village, but when the information was gathered, the volunteer genealogists were quickly able to find matches to members of the couple's families who had uploaded their own DNA profiles. Tracking back through the family trees of those matches, the volunteers identified the Sumter Does.

On January 21, 2021, the Sumter County Sheriff's Office and the DNA Doe Project held a press conference to announce that, after forty-four years, Sumter Jane and John/Jock Doe had names: Pamela Mae Buckley from Colorado Springs, Colorado, and James Paul Freund from Lancaster,

The Sumter Does identified, with sketches by volunteer forensic artist Carl William Koppelman. *Courtesy of DNA Doe Project and Carl William Koppelman via Wikimedia Commons.*

Pennsylvania. They'd both dropped contact with their families in December 1975, eight months before their bodies were found.

Both were older than at first assumed: Pamela was twenty-five; Paul was thirty. He'd been married, served in the army, had a child and filed for divorce. According to research by Columbia reporter Brittany Breeding, Pamela had been a local beauty queen and also toured the West Coast with a folk-singing trio called Sunlending, playing concerts and coffeehouses.

Where Pamela and Paul met, where they traveled, how they came to be in Sumter County and how they died soon after eating fruit ice cream—those questions aren't yet answered. But at least they have names. Their families requested privacy.

For the Sumter County Sheriff's Office, the murder cases remain open. Investigators hope keeping the case in the public eye will jog a memory or a conscience and bring them the lead they need.

For more on the pioneers in the art and science of genetic genealogy, see Edward Humes's *The Forever Witness: How DNA and Genealogy Solved a Cold Case Double Murder* (2022), on work by CeCe Moore and Parabon NanoLabs, and Barbara Rae-Venter's *I Know Who You Are: How an Amateur DNA Sleuth Unmasked the Golden State Killer and Changed Crime Fighting Forever* (2023).

CALIFORNIA COP KILLER

At first glance, the story of the tragic death of two young police officers in Los Angeles could have little place among the Palmetto State's crime stories, but what started on a hot California night in July 1957 ended more than two thousand miles away and forty-five years later in a retirement neighborhood near Columbia.

On that midsummer night in 1957, two teenaged couples were parked on a lonely lover's lane east of El Segundo when a man threatened them with a pistol. In a television interview decades later, one of the young men said he rolled down the window for some fresh air, then "the gun—that was my whole life in that millisecond."

The stranger ordered the four of them out of the car, robbed them, told them to disrobe, tied them up, raped the fifteen-year-old girl and drove off in their 1949 Ford, leaving the teens in the dark near an oil-tank farm. The girls' skirts were still on the back floorboard of the car.

Ninety minutes later, the Ford stopped at a red light on Sepulveda Boulevard in the beachside town southwest of LA. Then, for no clear reason, the driver ran the light—right in front of a patrol car. Officers Richard Phillips and Milton Curtis pulled the driver over. Almost immediately, another car with two officers pulled up to offer assistance. The driver had stepped out of the car and seemed cooperative, nothing more than an ordinary traffic stop. With the situation under control, Phillips and Curtis waved away the backup.

Left alone among the eucalyptus trees with the two officers, the driver surprised them with a small .22-caliber revolver. He shot them both and raced away. Phillips managed to fire three shots at the car and to radio for help.

The two officers who had stopped to assist moments before responded quickly to the scene. They found Curtis on the driver's seat of the patrol car and Phillips lying on the road, his citation book open on the patrol car's hood with only the date written in. Both were dead, shot three times each.

Police found the teenagers' Ford abandoned four blocks away, with two bullet holes in the back window and one in the car's trunk. They found two of Phillips's bullets inside the car but couldn't find the third one.

Later, after a watchman discovered the teens, police realized they were looking for the same man for both of that night's crimes. And from the teens, they now had a description: six feet tall, 190 pounds, with a slow-talking drawl.

As in any case involving the killing of one of their own, officers worked tirelessly, following up thousands of leads, but they could identify no suspect. When interviewed about the case years later, fingerprint specialist Howard Speaks said he knew how important his search of the Ford would be. He was disappointed when the rearview mirror yielded no usable prints. That was usually a good bet, since a thief often has to readjust the mirror. Speaks did, though, find two partials on the steering wheel, both apparently from the left thumb. He painstakingly matched the key points on the two until he fit them together into a full print. Having two partials to form a full print was a rarity. When they compared that print—which was done by hand in those days—to thousands of prints, they found no match.

True Detective magazine covered the case in 1958, which brought it to a national audience, but the police had no more leads for three years.

In April 1959, two years after the attacks and the officers' murders, a man working in his backyard uncovered the frame of a revolver with a missing cylinder. He put it on a shelf and thought no more about it. A year later, while doing some clean-up and tilling in his backyard, he unearthed a watch and a gun cylinder. When he found that the cylinder fit the frame, he took the nine-shot Harrington & Richardson .22-caliber revolver to the police.

The homeowner's backyard lay between where the stolen car was abandoned and Manhattan Beach. After ditching the Ford, the killer had apparently dodged over fences and through backyards to avoid being tracked, dropping his gun and loot in the process.

Ballistics connected the weapon to the murders. The serial number showed the gun had been purchased in 1957 for thirty dollars at a Sears store in Shreveport, Louisiana, by a large man with a southern accent. The teens who'd been attacked said the man had been gentlemanly and had apologized; perhaps he was from the South. The same man had signed a registration card to stay at the YMCA across the street from Sears, using the name George D. Wilson. But the fake name and fake address on the two registration forms meant the promising lead went nowhere.

The case went cold for decades, until California police got a tip in September 2002 that a woman's uncle claimed he'd killed the officers.

That tip proved yet another among thousands of false leads, but it prompted a new look at the case. The FBI's IAFIS (Integrated Automated Fingerprint Identification System), a nationwide searchable fingerprint database, opened for business in 1999. For the first time, investigators could compare prints from jurisdictions across the country. By 2002, the Los Angeles District Attorney's Office had three thousand unsolved homicides, dating back to 1980, that might benefit from the new tool.

With that many cases, though, the department hadn't looked farther back than a couple of decades—until the erroneous tip gave them a reason to look again at those two 1957 murders. They found their answer. Thanks to prints taken after a 1956 burglary arrest in South Carolina, California investigators made a breakthrough. In a stroke of good timing, South Carolina had added its fingerprint database to IAFIS only two months earlier. Now into the fifth decade of this murder investigation, authorities finally had a name: Gerald Fiten Mason. He'd served eight months of a three-year sentence for home breaking and larceny in South Carolina. After his release in 1957, he hitchhiked cross-country to California.

On the way, Mason stopped in Shreveport, where he signed two registration cards as "George D. Wilson," to stay at the YMCA and to purchase the gun at the nearby Sears. Once they had his real name, a handwriting expert used the latest technology to compare those two signatures against more recent exemplars, showing all were written by one man: Gerald Mason. The examiner commented that Mason's signature, surprisingly, hadn't changed over the years.

Mug shot of Gerald Mason taken in South Carolina after his 1956 arrest for burglary. *Courtesy of South Carolina public records.*

Since 1960, when Mason returned to South Carolina, he'd married, lived in a house in a quiet Cayce neighborhood and settled into life owning and running several gas stations. Mason was that most unexpected of killers—the one who committed no other violent act. Other than the burglary and the night of crime in California, sixty-eight-year-old Mason apparently led a comfortable life, married, working, raising a family, retiring to a nice house north of Columbia.

Now, investigators had a fingerprint and a handwriting match, but they wanted to make sure of their identification. They didn't want any oversight to derail their case.

When asked, a teenaged robbery victim couldn't identify Mason's 1957 photo in a lineup, but one of the officers who'd been waved away during the traffic stop identified the old photo of Mason as the man who'd stepped out of the Ford. Local police kept Mason under surveillance before U.S. marshals and officers from South Carolina and California moved in for the arrest on a fugitive warrant for robbery, rape, kidnapping and murder.

Neighbors who'd known Mason for decades couldn't believe police had the right man. Surely it was a mistake. In his retirement neighborhood, he was known as a handyman who helped his neighbors, who bowled, played golf and took trips to nearby Lake Murray.

In an interview with James Broder in the *New York Times*, one neighbor said, "What gets me is why would it take so many years to find somebody who has been so well known here in Columbia? It's not like he was living like a fugitive, hiding or running away from something."

The clincher in the case came when they got Mason in custody and asked him to remove his shirt. Detectives finally found what happened to the missing third bullet Officer Phillips had fired at the fleeing car that night. Mason had a scar on his right shoulder where Phillips's bullet struck him.

In interviews after his capture, Mason told investigators he'd bought the gun in Shreveport for protection while he was hitchhiking. When asked about the rape, he said he didn't remember why he did it. He shot the two policemen to protect himself: "I thought, 'If I don't get them, they're gonna get me.' So when the officer turned away from me, I shot both officers, got back in the car and drove away."

At his court hearing, Mason sobbed as he spoke: "I do not understand why I did this. It is contrary to everything I believe in and does not fit in my life. It is not the person I know. I detest these crimes." Mason pleaded guilty to the murders to save his family and friends from the ordeal of a trial and from reliving the worst part of his life. The other charges were dropped, and he was allowed to serve his time in South Carolina, to be closer to family.

Mason died in prison in 2017, just days before he would have turned eighty-three.

2

THE MISSING (AND FOUND)

THE SHAW CREEK KILLER

Some crime stories unfold so slowly, spread out over time and into different jurisdictions, that sometimes investigators can't spot the links, can't realize that separate crime scenes are part of a single, puzzling, tragic whole.

To better connect crimes and criminals, law enforcement consistently seeks ways to improve the flow of information. In 1924, the FBI began maintaining crime data using "pen and paper, index cards, and typewriters," according to its website, and in 1967, the FBI officially launched the first national crime reporting database, capturing information on "wanted and missing persons and stolen property." Records collection moved slowly because it relied on local and state investigators finding the time and resources to input the data—even when those investigators didn't always see any practical purpose to it. But by its fiftieth anniversary, the FBI system handled fourteen million transactions every day and served more than ninety thousand law enforcement and criminal justice agencies.

Sometimes, though, despite improved technology, patterns of crime can escape notice—unless a case piques one curious person's interest.

Micheal Whelan became interested in a series of unsolved murders and unidentified victims in the area around Aiken County, South Carolina, and Augusta, Georgia. He had studied broadcast journalism at Washington State University's Edward R. Murrow College of Communication, so he brought old-school journalism techniques to the newer technology of podcasting.

Podcasts are one of the more recent changes in the investigation and spread of crime stories among a growing audience. The first podcast was released in 2004; the first broadly popular true crime podcast, *Serial*, began airing ten years later. Almost twenty years after the first podcast, at least 1,200 true crime podcasts existed, making it one of the most popular podcast genres.

In Whelan's *Unresolved* podcast, he provides in-depth coverage of crime cases from across the United States, with occasional forays abroad. Some of his cases are in the international headlines—like the highly publicized murders of two young teens walking along an abandoned railroad bridge in Delphi, Indiana; an arrest was made in that case. Other cases he covers remain little-known and unsolved, including four cases in Aiken County.

Scant information was available about the murders when he started digging. His research initially focused on two victims—publicly known as the Aiken Does—but after studying other unsolved crimes in the area, he believed at least four cases were linked.

Whelan said in his podcast program notes, "So, without sounding too full of myself, I took it upon myself to put a name to this unknown killer: the Shaw Creek Killer. I think that's how we help raise awareness that whoever he or she is, they have at least four victims to their name and have never been brought to justice."

Crime scenes are no respecters of jurisdictional boundaries, and that is one of the elements that hid the links between these cases. The area around Aiken, North Augusta and Augusta covers several counties in the two states of South Carolina and Georgia. Residents in the region—and criminals and victims—move easily across the artificial borders. Augusta, on the western side of the Savannah River, is the region's big city, with a population of 200,000. Every year during the first week in April, its Augusta National Golf Club attracts golfers and fans from around the world to the Masters Tournament.

On the South Carolina side of the Savannah, the towns are small, cozy and very southern. Aiken's horse farms and polo fields have made it famous as South Carolina's Thoroughbred Country. Much of the area is rural, with pine forests and fields. Interstate 20 runs from Florence, South Carolina, through Columbia to Augusta, on its way to Atlanta and westward. The Shaw Creek area where the bodies were found lies about five miles north of the interstate highway.

For the Augusta area, the podcast *The Fall Line* first brought national attention to the unsolved cases of missing twin sisters—the only case of missing twins remaining unsolved, thirty years after they disappeared. The

View of the dense woods along Shaw Creek in Aiken County. *Courtesy of Andy Hunter.*

Oxygen network presented a documentary on the case, in which former federal prosecutor Laura Coates discusses the role and effect of podcasters in cold-case investigation:

> *Podcasts kind of fill in the gap from the cases that are on the verge of being cold or are already cold and reigniting the flame. And podcasts do it in a way that brings national attention; they are able to get the in-depth story and get people to feel and understand that these are actual human beings....That really appeals to people who want to do something but aren't in law enforcement.*

Prosecutor Coates acknowledged the benefits and risks of citizen-sleuths and podcasts:

> *Being a podcaster and its impact on an investigation is kind of a double-edged sword. On the one hand, it's a great thing because they have a level of naivete that makes them explore other areas they* [law enforcement] *wouldn't think of, they have a fresh perspective, they're not going to be*

hardened by something or be calloused, maybe, just be apathetic because they've seen it so much. They're going to have a different zeal. That's great, on the one hand.

On the other hand, because they're not trained about law enforcement tactics, about strategies, about interrogation, sometimes they open up conspiracy theories that otherwise would not have been there or taint the jury pool, if there ever were one. So on the one hand, it's great. On the other hand, there are some real shortcomings. But either way, at the end of the day, getting interest in a case can be more powerful than getting it right every time.

The missing twins—Dannette and Jeannette Millbrook—lived with their mother and several siblings in Augusta. The twins were only fifteen, while the women found in the vicinity of South Carolina's Shaw Creek ranged in age from late twenties to early thirties (though one could've been as young as late teens). Despite the differences, the Millbrook girls and the Shaw Creek victims shared some painful similarities: all were young Black women and the press provided very little coverage of their cases—at least until the podcasters started talking to people and digging into files.

While *The Fall Line* investigated the Augusta twins, Micheal Whelan turned his journalism training and curiosity to the Shaw Creek victims. He dug into and made public more information on these four women than any other writer or podcaster.

What was known about these four victims? And were their murders linked?

Victim 1, Aiken County Jane Doe 1987. On November 16, 1987, two hunters moving through deep woods found skeletal remains near Shaw Creek, in an area more than a mile south of where Johnston Highway and Mount Calvary Road cross and south of the town of Eureka. The body was placed face down, its legs crossed and arms outstretched, reminiscent of a crucifix. One officer thought the body looked posed. No clothes, jewelry or personal possessions were found nearby. Plant growth near the body, the intertwining of roots with the bones, the lack of any soft tissue and absence of recent insect activity all suggested the body had been there for anywhere from one to five years, so she likely disappeared during the years between 1982 and 1986.

As is common in a shallow burial in a wooded area, some bones were missing, likely from animal scavengers or the effects of weather and time. One foot was gone, and five of her teeth were missing, likely naturally detached after her body began to skeletonize. The hyoid bone—a horseshoe-shaped bone unattached to other bones and located in the front of the throat, which, when broken, can indicate strangulation—was not found. But the hyoid is a small and delicate bone and easily lost.

To help with the complex forensic aspects, Aiken County investigators asked South Carolina's State Law Enforcement Division (SLED) to bring its agents' expertise to search and assess the scene. Aiken County coroner Sue Townsend was also hands-on in the search. Scanning the scene with a metal detector, they located a brass shotgun shell casing underneath the body, described as lacking the plastic or paper casing of more modern shells.

A forensic exam determined that the female was Black but also possibly with Asian, East Indian or Caribbean ancestors. She was relatively tall for a woman—five feet, eight inches—and likely weighed between 150 and 160 pounds. She had some old, healed fractures on the left side of her nose and to her right knee. A right-side molar had been extracted long enough before death that the bony socket had healed. In life, her top teeth would have protruded noticeably over her bottom teeth. Judging from her bones, she could have been anywhere from seventeen to thirty years old—the widest age estimate of any of the Shaw Creek victims.

Tests of her hair revealed cocaine (though later academic research would show testing hair for cocaine use had limitations). That finding led to investigating missing sex workers or drug users in the two-state region. Some speculated she might have come from a migrant camp working the peach crop.

In July 1989, using the skull as the underlying model, a facial reconstruction was done. Reconstruction experts or sculptors can attach standard skin-thickness markers to the skull on which to mold a good approximation of the shape of the head and face, but they have to make educated guesses about certain features: Did she wear glasses? What shape and size were her lips and ears? Her eye color? The very things that help us recognize people we know could easily be missing or—even worse—re-created in a way that made the reconstruction unfamiliar to those who'd known her in life.

The investigators had little evidence. And it yielded no leads. They couldn't match her to any women reported missing in the early to mid-1980s.

Facial reconstruction of 1987 Aiken Doe by the National Center for Missing and Exploited Children. *Courtesy of NamUs and the Doe Network.*

VICTIM 2. On November 10, 1986, Jacquelyn "Jackie" Council dropped her five-year-old son off at school and disappeared. Thirty-year-old Jackie was reported missing that same day. Her body wasn't found until more than four years later, in the same wooded area south of Eureka. Though her remains were found in March 1991, they weren't definitively identified until 1999.

In 1997, in an attempt to confirm the possible identity of the March 1991 bones, a pathologist at the University of South Carolina superimposed Jackie's photograph onto an image of the skull. By matching the eye sockets, facial bones and other bony markers, investigators knew they had found Jackie Council.

The superimposition technique was first used in the United Kingdom in 1936, to identify two bodies chopped into bits, wrapped in sheets and old clothes and scattered off a bridge into the waters of what Scottish locals called the Devil's Beef Tub. It took authorities a while to gather enough of the grisly parcels to realize they had two female bodies. The killer, adept with a scalpel and other surgical tools, had removed the noses, ears, fingers and toes—anything that might help identify the corpses. Forensic pathologist John Glaister Jr. and anatomist James Brash took hours piecing the bodies together in order to identify them. The work was so groundbreaking, they detailed it in an illustrated book, *Medico-Legal Aspects of the Ruxton Case.* But who were the two women?

The notion of using photography and X-rays to superimpose photographs of missing Isabella Ruxton over one of the skulls was novel. It required capturing the image of the skull in the same pose as a photograph of the suspected victim. In 1936, those graphic images and Dr. Glaister's detailed testimony were enough to convict Dr. Buck Ruxton, an obstetrician who practiced in England near the border with Scotland, of murdering his wife and their young housemaid, Mary Rogerson.

According to *Time* magazine, the trial of the popular doctor caused such a sensation that a dedicated telephone switchboard was linked to the London

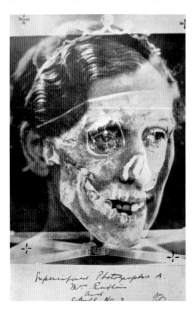

Superimposition of photograph and victim's skull helped convict England's Dr. Buck Ruxton in 1936. *Reprinted in Notable British Trials'* Trial of Buck Ruxton *(1937).*

press, "just like in America," and the judge excused the jurors from jury service "for the rest of your lives because of the dreadful and gruesome details you have been forced to hear."

By the late 1990s, DNA had become the gold standard for identification. Because superimposed images require a degree of subjective judgment, in 1999, investigators compared DNA from Shaw Creek's second victim with DNA from Jackie's son to confirm the identity made with the superimposed image. Thirteen years after she disappeared, using two landmark forensic techniques, the remains of Jackie Council were conclusively identified.

VICTIM 3. Risteen Durden disappeared on March 13, 1989, from her hometown in Avera, Georgia, southwest of Augusta. Her remains were found in March 1992, a little over an hour from Avera, dumped near a pond off Uncle Duck Road in Aiken County, about fifteen miles from the Shaw Creek area. The distance from the other locations meant this case wasn't initially linked to the Shaw Creek victims.

Hoping someone would recognize her, investigators provided the sketch from a facial reconstruction of the skull to the Augusta newspaper. This time, it worked. A family member saw the photo, and in February 1993, dental records confirmed Risteen Durden's identity.

A month later, a group of University of South Carolina–Columbia forensic anthropology students helped Coroner Sue Townsend and some officers search the area near Uncle Duck Road; they located bone fragments but nothing to help find the killer.

Authorities stated she'd died of gunshot wounds but haven't officially linked her with the Shaw Creek victims. Certain elements suggest her death is related: a twenty-nine-year-old Black woman found nude with no clothes or possessions nearby, dumped in the same vicinity as three similar victims.

VICTIM 4, AIKEN COUNTY JANE DOE 1993. On January 25, 1993, less than one year after Risteen Durden was found, timber company employees working in the pine woods south and east of Eureka and Highways 191 and 208 came across another skeleton. She was found within a half mile of where Jane Doe 1987 and Jackie Council were found. Like the others, this body was nude, with no money, clothing or personal possessions nearby. As with Jane Doe 1987, one to five years was the closest estimate of the time since death, putting her disappearance and death somewhere between 1988 and 1992.

Once again, the corpse offered no clear leads to the victim's identity or to the killer.

This victim was killed by an injury to the back of her neck—either a stab wound or perhaps a gunshot, judging from the damage to her bones. A fire had burned the vegetation and ground around her body, perhaps after a lapse of time during which the body partially decomposed. No shotgun shells or other projectiles or potential weapons were found.

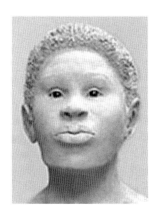

Facial reconstruction of 1993 Aiken Doe created by Billy Aiken. *Courtesy of the Doe Network.*

The mostly skeletal remains and the burning of the body made identification and analysis of the cause of death more difficult. From the bones, investigators could tell she was between twenty-five and thirty-five years old and was between five feet, four inches and five feet, seven inches in height. Her bones indicated she was right-handed. As with Jane Doe 1987, her front teeth protruded noticeably.

As with the others, the death likely occurred elsewhere, which made yet more evidence irretrievable. An extensive search of the area by Coroner Townsend and other investigators located a tooth and some additional bone fragments but nothing that answered their questions.

POSSIBLE VICTIMS OF SHAW CREEK KILLER

Victim	Date found	Date missing	Date identified
#1 Aiken Doe 1987	Nov. 16, 1987	1982–1986	unidentified
#2 Jackie Council	March 1991	Nov. 10, 1986	1997 & 1999
#3 Risteen Durden	March 1992	March 13, 1989	Feb. 1993
#4 Jane Doe 1993	Jan. 25, 1993	1988–1992	unidentified

According to podcaster Micheal Whelan's research, the names of killers operating in the area with possible links to these unsolved murders included:

JOSEPH PATRICK WASHINGTON. Convicted of violent rapes, kidnapping and robbery for crimes against young Black women in Augusta, he never stood trial for murdering two victims because he died in prison, possibly from AIDS complications. Those women were shot in the head, which might not match the

Shaw Creek killings. Did he also kidnap Dannette and Jeannette Millbrook? He was a viable suspect, given the area where he preyed on victims.

JOHN WAYNE BOYER. With his flowing beard and his three-hundred-pound frame, he could have been Santa Claus, but instead, he was arrested as the Long-Haul Territory Killer in 2007. Boyer lived with his mother in Augusta, and he traveled the country as a trucker. Along the way, he murdered at least three women. In 2007, he pleaded guilty to second-degree murder for the death of a woman from eastern North Carolina, whom he claimed died of a drug overdose.

After his relatively short twelve-year sentence in that case, DNA matches linked him to other murders in Tennessee and in South Carolina, where a woman's body was found near Interstate 20 outside Florence. He was sentenced to what will likely become a life sentence in Tennessee. Podcaster Whelan pointed out that Boyer's victims were white, while the Shaw Creek victims were Black. And Boyer dumped his victims in widespread locations away from his Augusta home, making him an unlikely suspect in the Aiken case, in which the bodies were located not far from Augusta.

FRANK THANIEL POTTS. A migrant worker who lived and traveled through the Carolinas, Georgia and further south, Potts served time for molesting children, kidnapping a game warden and killing a young man whose body was found near Potts's off-the-grid cabin in Alabama. Aiken authorities received tips about him, but he was in prison during the time span of the Shaw Creek killings.

No other likely suspects have been named. Podcaster Micheal Whelan said, in a poignant summary of the case, "I wish I could do and say more, but for the time being, the stories of Jackie Council, Risteen Durden and the Aiken Jane Does remain…unresolved."

SNATCHED FROM HER BED

On the night of June 6, 1986, four-year-old Jessica Gutierrez—Jessie, to her family and friends—was taken from her bedroom, and she has never been found.

Jessie's six-year-old sister told investigators that she'd seen the man who took her little sister from their bedroom and that he wore a "magic hat." That description was all investigators had to work with.

The mystery of what happened to Jessie remained unsolved—though from the very beginning, Jessie's mother, Debbie Gutierrez-Garnsey, had a suspect in mind, someone she knew from West Columbia, a convicted sex offender. Some cases take time to build, though. Investigators and solicitors are too aware of the risks of bringing a defendant to trial too quickly. If jurors fail to see evidence that convinces them beyond a reasonable doubt, a killer may walk free and cannot again be prosecuted, even if better evidence is later discovered.

But the risks of making a mistake don't set aside the heartbreak and the sense of injustice. In Jessie's case, a public exchange between two legendary Lexington County law enforcement officials erupted twenty years after she disappeared. In 2007 interviews with WIS News 10's Kara Gormley, longtime solicitor Donnie Myers (first elected to the office in 1977) squared off against longtime county sheriff James Metts (first elected in 1972). Gormley reported that the sheriff said the solicitor was not prosecuting the case, that they hadn't been able "to convince the solicitor that we need to move forward as far as prosecution is concerned."

Solicitor Myers countered, pointing out that he's not the one who issues arrest warrants—and no one had been arrested. Meyers said he would take the evidence to a grand jury once an arrest was made. "We'll throw at it whatever we got."

But no one had been arrested in the two decades since Jessie disappeared. Reading between the lines of the interviews with Gormley, a likely suspect had emerged quickly. But the little girl's body was never found, and convincing evidence of guilt was apparently lacking. Evaluating how a case was investigated decades ago is always skewed by what is currently possible, given the advances in forensic science. As perspective, the first DNA prosecution in the United States was still a year away when Jessie was kidnapped. In that first case, DNA helped convict a rapist in Florida. In the late 1980s, touch DNA, cellphone tower pings and genetic genealogy would've sounded like futuristic science fiction.

In a murder case, not having a body makes the case more difficult to prosecute—not impossible, but certainly difficult. Is the victim actually dead? How and when did she die? What evidence connects the suspect with the death? Those elements can be difficult to prove even when a body has been found.

In a homicide, evidence from the victim's body is often key, but other evidence can also establish the *corpus delicti* or the legal "body of the case." While a handful of no body trials have made headlines in the last few decades, the results were sometimes controversial and occasionally overturned on appeal.

The "no body, no murder" rule, like most legal rules, was prompted by precedent. The U.S. experience with no body cases reaches back to an 1819 Vermont case where two brothers were convicted of killing their brother-in-law, even though his body wasn't found.

But in an odd resurrection, he was later located in New Jersey, healthy and alive—and fortunately before the brothers were hanged. Questions were raised, though, about whether the resurrected brother-in-law was actually an imposter who conveniently "appeared" in order to free the killers. In former U.S. assistant attorney Tad DiBiase's excellent online listing of no body cases (see references), this is the earliest U.S. prosecution he's located.

For the original no body case, most reports point to the disappearance of seventy-year-old William Harrison in 1660. William disappeared from Chipping Campden, England. Only later would he become known as the Campden Wonder.

William's coat and bloodstained shirt collar were found on a roadside, but no one could locate the elderly man. Likely under intense—perhaps violent—questioning, William's servant John Perry admitted that he saw his own brother and his mother rob and kill William and dump his body in a pond. Dutifully, the authorities drained the pond but found no body. No matter. They had an eyewitness—who must also be complicit—so all three of the Perrys were hanged months later, in 1661.

The next year, William Harrison miraculously returned home very much alive and bearing a wild tale: he'd been kidnapped by Barbary pirates, sold into slavery in Turkey and only recently escaped.

Following William's astounding resurrection from the dead and the judicial deaths of three innocent people, England adopted the no body, no murder rule, all the better to avoid such outcomes in the future—or at least for almost three hundred years. In the mid-twentieth century, England and the United States once again allowed no body prosecutions, in the words of a 1960 California case, when evidence "sufficient to exclude every other reasonable hypothesis, may prove the death of a missing person, the existence of a homicide and the guilt of the accused." Prosecutions without a body were again an option.

Given the challenges of gathering enough evidence to not only prove that a homicide has happened (which is usually simple if the body is present) but also prove who did it beyond a reasonable doubt, prosecutors are still sometimes reluctant to take on a case with no body. After all, prosecutors must use their scarce resources wisely and must balance the number of untried cases against the odds of winning a difficult conviction.

Solicitor Myers had successfully prosecuted a no body case, but he said, "It has to be a mountain of evidence when there is [a] no body case. There has to be a volume of evidence." But Myers also told WIS News 10, "Never have I told anyone in any case not to arrest someone. That's not my job."

Both Metts and Myers were known as colorful, no-holds-barred characters who dominated the criminal justice scene in Lexington County for decades. When the reporter again followed up with Myers one month after her initial 2007 interview, he bluntly stated that in South Carolina, arresting someone is only part of the case. A prosecutor also needs evidence to prove the case in court. "You don't take a switch blade into a gun fight.…I wouldn't put myself in that position to go into a courtroom when I've got a knife, someone else has a bazooka or a shot gun."

A SLED spokesman said Sheriff Metts had requested their assistance on the case, searching anew for Jessie. Though the statement didn't spell out what that assistance involved, SLED can provide local investigators with technical and lab support to analyze crime scene evidence, among other services. Reports said the FBI was also involved, through its Child Abduction Rapid Deployment Team, with as many as ten FBI field offices assisting.

Whatever was happening behind the scenes in this case, the investigation seemed to lag again until news broke in January 2022 that a sixty-one-year-old suspect had been arrested in Wake County, North Carolina, on warrants from Lexington County. He was charged with murder, kidnapping and first-degree burglary.

In his preliminary hearing in March 2022, the prosecutors said the accused told other inmates he'd been responsible for Jessie's disappearance. Her body has not been found, and no trial date has been set as of this writing.

The Survivor Who Thrived

Thanks to the survivor who thrived, a killer's story was eclipsed by his would-be victim's resilience. On June 22, 2002, fifteen-year-old Kara Robinson was watering flowers outside a friend's house when a man pulled up, started a conversation to make sure no adults were home and then held a gun to the side of her neck and forced her into a large plastic bin he had ready in the back seat of his green Pontiac Firebird.

To her family, she'd vanished in broad daylight. To Kara, it was the start of an eighteen-hour nightmare, bound and held captive in a Columbia apartment.

Kara was determined to keep track of where she was and who she was with, and took note of everything: the serial number on the plastic bin, the lizards and fish displayed in his apartment living room, the long red hairs in the hairbrush on the bathroom counter.

She engaged her abductor in conversation, offered to do housework, refused to let him see her cry and seemed to win at least a bit of trust. To herself, she kept reciting a refrain: "Gather information. Wait for him to be complacent. Escape."

When he finally fell asleep, she quietly slipped one wrist free of the handcuffs, freed her ankle of its restraint, flung open the front door and ran for help. She flagged down a driver who took her to the Richland County Sheriff's Office, the handcuff still dangling from her wrist.

Her detailed descriptions, with help from the apartment maintenance man, led police to the door of Richard Marc Evonitz, a married thirty-eight-year-old navy veteran with a job and, on the surface, an ordinary life. He'd held Kara in the apartment he shared with his wife while she was out of town.

Kara's resourcefulness didn't just save her life—it provided answers for the families of three girls in Spotsylvania County, Virginia: Sofia Silva, who was kidnapped from her front steps and murdered in 1996, and sisters Kristin

South Carolina Law Enforcement Division headquarters in Columbia. *Photo by Cathy Pickens.*

and Kati Lisk, also abducted and found murdered in 1997. The girls had been dumped in flowing water in hopes of destroying evidence. *America's Most Wanted* featured the Lisk sisters' case six times in the five years between their deaths and Kara Robinson's 2002 escape. A news clipping found in a footlocker in Evonitz's apartment pointed Richland County sheriff Leon Lott to the connection with the Pennsylvania murders.

As soon as Kara ran from his apartment, Evonitz took off, but police weren't far behind. They tracked him to Florida and, after a high-speed chase, cornered him at the waterfront in Sarasota. When police surrounded him, he shot and killed himself.

Kara Robinson said she was disappointed she didn't get to face him in court. "I wanted him to look at me and know that choosing me was the biggest mistake he ever made."

While in high school, Kara worked with victim services and in a DNA lab. After college, she attended the South Carolina Criminal Justice Academy, and in 2010, eight years after her ordeal, she walked across the stage as the only female graduate in her class. She worked as a school resource officer and in investigations, focusing on sexual assault, child abuse and victim services. She left law enforcement to raise her children and work as a motivational speaker. Kara Robinson Chamberlin's website: https://www. kararobinsonchamberlain.com.

3

THE LADY KILLERS

BEATRICE SNIPES

In a threat that could've been growled by an actor in a badly written 1930s black-and-white movie, the law told Beatrice Snipes it would be in her best interest to get out of town. In July 1932, after one too many trips through police court in Columbia, Beatrice and her husband, Clyde, decided to take the law's kind offer: move on somewhere else and she wouldn't have to pay the $10 fine (about $200 today) for her latest disorderly conduct charge.

The two textile mill workers decided Danville, Virginia, sounded like a nice place to settle. One version of the story had them heading out for the promised land of Virginia on July 17, 1932, but on that date, they were traveling with another couple who lived in Fort Mill to visit Clyde's dying stepmother in Charlotte.

Clyde was driving their companions' Ford roadster on two-lane Highway 21 when they passed an oncoming Dodge coupe. The driver of the coupe turned around and pursued them. In the spirit of "can't catch a break," the Snipeses and their friends were pulled over for speeding by York County rural police officer Elliott Harris about two football fields' length from the North Carolina state line. Harris's Dodge was driven by another Fort Mill native and Furman University student, Kenyon Young.

Officer Harris was diligent about keeping an eye out for illegal liquor being transported toward Charlotte, upholding the Prohibition-era laws whenever he could. Reports didn't mention whether he knew of Clyde's history running bootleg liquor, but Clyde wasn't hauling any that day. Clyde also didn't have a driver's license.

Some altercation over the lack of a license compounded the speeding charge. Beatrice later said she felt threatened by Officer Harris. Formal accounts said Clyde refused to get into the officer's car, and when a scuffle ensued, Harris pulled his gun. But Kenyon Young, the ride-along college student and the witness closest to the fray, said Beatrice was the one who came up behind Harris and pulled his gun from its holster. In whatever manner the fight unfolded, it ended when Beatrice shot the officer in the leg with his own gun. At the inquest, Kenyon Young said Harris had his arm around her neck as his leg collapsed under his weight. The next shots hit his head, chest and his leg.

Officer Harris had taken the keys to the roadster Clyde was driving when he searched it for illegal liquor. Without the keys to start his friend's car, Clyde and Beatrice escaped in the officer's coupe.

Officer Harris was badly injured but alive. The Snipeses' male traveling companion helped lift Harris into the Ford roadster and drove with Kenyon to find medical care.

To compound the tragedy, a local man raced to find Mrs. Harris and tell her the news so she could be with her husband. He left Rock Hill riding a motorcycle borrowed from Officer Harris's house, crashed into the back of a car and fatally broke his neck.

Officer Harris died that day, leaving his widow and four children between the ages of four months and six years old.

Clyde's stepmother died later that night, some say just moments after she heard news of the officer's shooting.

Beatrice soon turned herself in to the police in Charlotte, though Clyde stayed on the run a while longer. Officers took Beatrice to York, the county seat representing Fort Mill and Rock Hill. To be safe, the officers took a route west from Charlotte through Gastonia, rather than through Fort Mill. The couple was then moved farther away to the county jail in Chester because, as the news reported, "feeling was running high."

Clyde's only crime, after the dust settled, was stealing the officer's car ("driving a car without the consent of the owner," according to a news account). Beatrice, though, faced capital murder charges. The pair were held in the state penitentiary in Columbia before their trials—again, for safekeeping.

Four months later, on December 5, 1932, Beatrice stood trial in the York County Courthouse. The facts were not much in dispute, and the testimony concluded that day. The attorneys made their arguments before lunch the next day. After three hours of deliberation, the all-male jury found her guilty of murder—which meant she must be sentenced to die.

No one contended that she shouldn't be punished, but most court watchers believed the jury would recommend mercy, thereby giving her a life sentence. The reporter covering the trial for the *Yorkville Enquirer* (and reprinted in *The State* newspaper) expressed surprise:

> *The verdict is perhaps unique in Palmetto jurisprudence in all its connotations but nobody who heard the trial of the woman disputes the fact that the verdict was justified by the evidence and the law which makes no distinction between the sexes in this state.*
>
> *But that a jury of South Carolina men would follow the evidence and the law to its logical conclusion and not be swerved by the chivalry which used to be above the law and everything else in South Carolina was not believed by any of the court habitués before the verdict was rendered.*

Throughout the trial, Beatrice remained "as composed as the loser in a bridge game." Even when she heard the verdict, she remained stoic. Seated beside her, Clyde didn't take her verdict so calmly. "Snipes showed much more feeling than did his wife. At times his face showed great strain and the facial muscles became almost convulsive," said the *Yorkville* reporter. Clyde's sentence had already been given in court the previous day, but he was allowed to sit with his wife during her trial.

Her reaction when she was later sentenced had changed:

> *And it was a different Beatrice than the one who sustained so debonair, not to say sprightly, a demeanor throughout a long trial and a verdict of murder without recommendation for mercy not long ago.*
>
> *As she stood at the bar of the court she was amazed, befuddled, overwhelmed, lacking assurance for the first time dazed, unable to understand the catastrophe that engulfed her—but also mercifully benumbed beyond much suffering.*

Beatrice Snipes became the first woman in South Carolina sentenced to death in the electric chair, which had been in operation since 1912. Her execution date was set for April 7, 1933. That date would allow Beatrice time to give birth to the child she was carrying before she was put to death.

Condemning a pregnant woman to die two months before her due date set up an international hue and cry for commuting her sentence to life in

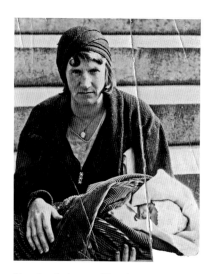

Beatrice Snipes and her baby in 1933.
Courtesy of Richland Library, Columbia, South Carolina.

prison. According to Mark Wineka's 2012 interview with Beatrice's daughter Jean, citizens in distant Holland had put twenty-three thousand signatures on a petition supporting Beatrice. An Arkansas woman offered to die in her place so Beatrice could raise her baby. At the time of her December 1932 trial, a singer named Bob Miller recorded "Beatrice Snipes" on the B-side of a 45-rpm record. Even attorney Clarence Darrow publicly supported her. Because she was pregnant at the time of the shooting, he pointed out, "You don't know what the state of mind she was in." Governor Ibra Blackwood was sensitive to the interests of the grieving families in York County, but notes of appreciation poured into his office when he commuted her sentence.

The baby was born and stayed with Beatrice in prison until she was seven months old. Then Beatrice's older sister, Hyacinth Summey, took the baby to raise on her farm in Lancaster, South Carolina.

Beatrice spent her prison time, first in the state penitentiary in downtown Columbia and, in 1938, in the newly opened women's prison at the Broad River Farm. She worked as an inspector in the prison sewing shop, did personal needlework that she sold to earn money and wrote letters to a passing line of governors asking about the welfare of her little baby.

Meanwhile, Clyde served his seven-month sentence and was released. He spent his freedom racking up drunk-and-disorderly charges in Columbia and Charlotte. Later, though, he followed Beatrice's advice and "found himself a good woman."

According to the *New York Daily News*, after years of working within the prison and selling her needlework on the side, writing poetry, saving her money and trying to live her Christian faith by helping other women navigate the difficulties of prison, Beatrice got another bad-news letter toward the end of 1944: the parole board had looked at her case and denied her request. She once again wrote the state's governor, this time Governor Olin Johnston. She told him that her son Clyde Jr. was fighting for his country in the U.S. Navy and how she'd watched others with life sentences get out in less time than she'd served. She said her result could be different "if I only had someone to fight my case as they have had." And she reminded him that she had a little girl out there waiting for her.

Beatrice's persistence paid off. On January 2, 1945, Governor Johnston's last official act in office was to reduce her sentence and provide for a full pardon. She would go to her sister's house and become young Jean Summey's Aunt Bea and not let her daughter know their true relationship. Later, of course, Beatrice couldn't keep that secret. She whispered to Jean that she was really her mother and that she'd fought hard for custody and to be in touch with her.

The *Daily News* opened its lengthy article on Beatrice's journey and her release by describing the change prison had wrought: "No one who saw her last in 1932 would recognize her in 1945. Then she was a friendless, dissipated, broken hag of 30. Now, in spite of her graying hair, she looks younger than her 43 years. She stands erect. The lines of drunkenness, prostitution, and general cussedness have gone from her face. Her blue eyes are bright and expectant—and with reason."

Years later, Beatrice's daughter Jean Summey Ghent told reporter Mark Wineka that Beatrice had given her a collection of news clippings about "Baby Snipes" and about the shooting. Jean also kept Beatrice's prison Bible and her much-used crochet hooks.

Beatrice Snipes narrowly escaped death. Had her daughter not saved her life, she would have taken from Sue Logue the honor of being the first woman to die in the state's electric chair. Had Professor T. Felder Dorn not dug into the archives of Beatrice's case and collaborated with her daughter, her story would have drifted from memory and been lost. In recounting Beatrice's story and in his thoroughly researched books on South Carolina murderesses Sue Logue (*The Guns of Meeting Street*, University of South Carolina Press, 2006) and May Walker Burleson (later in this chapter), Professor Dorn has preserved the stories behind the South Carolina women tried for murder. His book on Sue Logue precipitated his introduction to the Snipes case. After she read the book, one of Jean's granddaughters contacted him to ask if he knew "that Baby Snipes was alive and well and living in North Carolina?" From that, Dorn's research and Jean Ghent's family mementoes reconstructed the story of a family torn apart and put back together.

Rose Stinnette

A murderess is, statistically speaking, relatively rare. Still, the husband-killing case of Rose Stinnette (or Rosa Stinette, depending on the source) would not have attracted international attention based solely on her gender. This murder stood out, in part, for the number of accomplices Rose was able to enlist: she enticed four men—one, her boyfriend—to bludgeon her twenty-eight-year-old husband, Charles Stinnette, to death.

Forty-one-year-old Rose, originally from Williamsburg County, was known according to one source as a root doctor or natural healer. Had she used a spell or potion to inveigle them into killing Charles and dumping his body near the railroad track? Had she told them about the five (or eight, depending on the source) separate life insurance policies she'd taken out on Charles—among the twenty-odd small policies she held on a number of friends and acquaintances? She did, it turned out, pay her accomplices for their help.

On Friday evening, April 19, 1946, Rose and Charlie Stinnette, along with their boarder, forty-two-year-old Sam Frazier, and twenty-five-year-old Roy Singletary, caught the 9:10 p.m. train at the Lake City station, bound for Florence about thirty miles away. Reports of their statements made to the coroner didn't explain the purpose of the trip, but Florence was a larger town and offered options for shopping, eating, drinking and entertainment not available in their hometown of Lake City.

The quartet disembarked at the station and began walking along the railroad tracks away from downtown.

Considering what had happened six months earlier, Charlie might not have agreed to walk alone along train tracks with Singletary. Maybe he felt safer this time, with his wife along. The previous October, Stinnette had been walking with Singletary and another man—Foster Sparkman—when Singletary hit him in the head with a stick of wood. The two men stole Stinnette's clothes and left him lying near the tracks, apparently dead.

Stinnette surprised them by later appearing at Singletary's house, announcing someone tried to kill him. It was not reported how much clothing they'd left for him to wear on his walk from the tracks.

Rose's reaction after Stinnette showed up alive was to scold her two accomplices because they "messed it up."

On April 19, Charlie Stinnette was once again making his way along some railroad tracks, this time thirty miles from home, with Rose and Sam Frazier. Frazier had served time for murder, been released a little over a year earlier and started boarding with the Stinnettes. He'd also become

Rose's live-in lover—he described her as his sweetheart—though Charlie likely didn't know about that. Foster Sparkman stepped out from a hiding place along the track and hit Charlie in the head with "a three-foot-long piece of one-inch pine." According to the report, Charlie "rolled down the embankment, coming to rest face downward."

Rose and Singletary took the stick of wood and climbed down the hill, and each of them struck him. They turned him over, took $80, put his wallet back in his pocket and then stole his watch. They walked farther out of town before circling back along the road to the train station, where Rose and Singletary caught a cab back to Lake City. They could afford the luxury. The money they stole would be worth about $1,200 today.

A railroad worker spotted Stinnette's body a few hours later, just before dawn. Other rail workers were able to describe the threesome they'd seen walking the tracks about 9:30 the night before.

City police and sheriff's deputies from Florence and Lake City, the Florence County coroner and the head of the Atlantic Coast Line Railroad's police force immediately got to work solving the murder. They found the bloodstained pine stick thrown into a train car on the "stockyard siding." They discovered Charlie's hat on the tracks, identified three distinct wounds on his head and found indications that he'd been turned over and probably robbed.

When arrested, Sam Frazier had Charlie's wristwatch "cleverly concealed in a leather cigarette case under the cigarette package and further covered by a piece of cellophane."

Rose admitted she'd given Sparkman $10 and told him to get himself to Florence. After the murder, she paid Singletary $15 (about $150 and $225 today, respectively). Sparkman admitted his involvement in planning both attacks on Charlie but insisted he hadn't been anywhere near Florence that night.

The trial date came a scant two months after the murder. The local paper's gossipy Seen About Town column reported, along with news of visitors to town, a patient recovering in McLeod Infirmary and an upcoming civic meeting, some verbal quips from the court proceedings:

> *A court room almost full of spectators, sweltering the heart of the warmest day of 1946, listening intently and at times with high amusement to the trial of four defendants....*
>
> *Defense attorney Wylie Caldwell suffering particularly from the heat, as perspiration soaked through his coat to make him look as if he had been caught in a downpour.*

One witness becoming so confused in a cross-examination…[that] she started to leave the stand. At one point she was answering [Solicitor Reuben] Long's questions before he asked them.

Authorities took two months to bring the case to trial, which lasted two days. The jury deliberated three hours, giving its verdict on Friday afternoon.

Rose Stinnette and "stoop-shouldered" Roy Singletary were sentenced to death. The double death sentence marked a historic first for Florence. But as the local paper acknowledged, "such heinous crimes as the cold-blooded carefully planned, brutal slaying of Charlie Stinnette" were also historic—a murder that was planned, attempted, failed spectacularly and then accomplished six months later, after the killers had plenty of time to reconsider their actions.

Sam Frazier and Foster Sparkman, Rose's other two accomplices, were found guilty as accessories and given life sentences. Little or no evidence was introduced that they were at the scene of the murder or in Florence that night.

Rose was held in the Florence County jail until only days before her execution and, as described by the Florence paper, "at the end of that time will walk the last walk to an ugly old chair in a small windowless room in Columbia." Rose and Singletary were scheduled to be executed on January 3, but Governor Ransome Williams ordered two delays so he could study the case more carefully. Citing how Rose's statements had "exonerated him and that trial jurors and other Florence citizens had recommended clemency for him," the governor commuted Singletary's sentence to life two weeks after he'd originally been scheduled to die.

On January 21, 1947, Governor Williams's term ended. In a practice still common when state or federal executives leave office, prisoners' petitions for clemency were heard—and Williams granted four that were recommended by county solicitors, plus the traditional commutations for prisoners who worked as servants in the governor's mansion. The outgoing governor said the Probation and Parole Board had other cases under consideration, and if recommendations were made, he would sign those. But he didn't commute Rose Stinnette's sentence.

The incoming governor was Strom Thurmond, who five years earlier as a circuit court judge had been involved in breaking up the shootout in Edgefield that eventually led to the execution of Sue Logue, who became the first woman to die in South Carolina's electric chair. Logue was convicted of hiring a hitman to kill the store owner who'd shot her husband in an

South Carolina's electric chair, first in operation in 1912. *Courtesy of Richland Library, Columbia, South Carolina.*

altercation. (For more on that case, see *True Crime Stories of Upstate South Carolina*, The History Press, 2022.)

Rose tried "pleading the belly" to delay her execution. Under old English common law, a pregnant woman's execution could be delayed until she delivered her child. An X-ray revealed Rose wasn't pregnant. That ploy didn't win her any sympathy. Of the four convicted in Charlie Stinnette's bludgeoning death, only Rose went to the chair, the second—and the last woman—executed in South Carolina's electric chair. By comparison, since 1912, when responsibility for carrying out criminal punishments moved from the local counties to the state government, 282 men have been executed.

Twenty-five-year-old Roy Singletary, the third accomplice, had been sentenced to death but was reprieved by the governor and sentenced to life in prison.

That didn't sit well with Rose. From the execution room, she laid the crime at Roy Singletary's feet and defended her innocence. A *Pittsburgh Courier* article portrayed her unbowed last moments as she declared she hadn't killed her husband: "As she sat in the chair she told witnesses 'The man who killed him is on the chaingang.'"

Her execution made headlines around the country. In Spokane, Washington, the *Spokesman-Review* reported, "She entered the death chamber with a broad smile on her face, greeted the assembled officials and witnesses with a cheerful 'good morning, folks, how's everybody?' and showed no concern as she was strapped in the chair."

When the switch was thrown on the death chair, a fuse blew and the room went dark until, according to reports, someone lit a match. Witnesses saw sparks and smoke around Rose's head and arms.

In 2021, Rose's last moments were chronicled in an appeal from another Death Row inmate, Brad Keith Sigmon. The cocktail of drugs used in lethal injection executions was not available, and Sigmon's attorneys argued that the electric chair was an inhumane alternative. They cited a litany of South Carolina's electric chair horror stories—including Rose's—and argued that "South Carolina and every other death penalty jurisdiction have turned away from electrocution because of 'its specter of excruciating pain and its certainty of cooked brains and blistered bodies.' [Citations omitted.] By compelling Sigmon to die in their century-old electric chair, [officials] subject him to a substantial risk of excruciating pain, terror, and certain bodily mutilation that contravenes evolving standards of decency [and] offends basic principles of human dignity."

In 2021, South Carolina passed laws allowing the use of the electric chair if lethal injection was not available and also permitting an inmate to choose death by firing squad. In September 2022, a state judge issued a permanent injunction against use of either the electric chair or firing squad as unconstitutional.

JENNIE MAY WALKER BURLESON

From its opening in 1912, Columbia's Hotel Jefferson at 1801 Main Street provided the best in meals and lodging for decades, the place to meet and be seen in the capital city's downtown. On Friday, March 8, 1940, a tall, striking woman entered the hotel, spoke briefly with the assistant desk clerk and then took a seat in the lobby to smoke her cigarette and wait for someone—or something.

Hotel resident Isabel Reece Burleson entered the lobby from the street, checked with the clerk to see if she had any messages and proceeded to the hotel's dining room for lunch. She was the second wife of Colonel Richard C. Burleson, who was stationed at Camp Jackson after the post was reactivated for the army's World War II preparations. Since his transfer to Columbia four months before, she and her husband had lived at the Hotel Jefferson.

The woman who'd been smoking and waiting again approached the clerk. "Is that Mrs. Burleson? Mrs. Richard Burleson? In the green coat?" She used to know her, she said, years ago.

The clerk confirmed that was indeed the officer's wife.

The Hotel Jefferson stood at the corner of Columbia's Main and Laurel Streets. *Courtesy of R. Maxey Collection, Richland Library, Columbia, South Carolina.*

Interior of Hotel Jefferson, demolished in 1968. *Courtesy of R. Maxey Collection, Richland Library, Columbia, South Carolina.*

The tall woman, dressed in a black coat, sporting a little black hat and wearing a corsage of violets, followed the woman in the green coat to her table. Witnesses said she approached the table and leaned over Mrs. Burleson. With one hand grasping the back of a chair, she shoved her handbag into the middle of Mrs. Burleson's back.

Mrs. Burleson glanced up and screamed, in fear or surprise. Immediately, the closest witness heard the shot and saw the handgun "punched through the bag" with only a couple of inches of the barrel showing.

Next, the tall woman stepped around to face her victim and fired again. The second shot only grazed Mrs. Burleson's arm, but the first hit a major artery and nothing could be done to save her.

Diners reacted quickly to the scream and two gunshots. Professor William McCall, who had walked over from the University of South Carolina campus for lunch, managed to wrest the gun away. Others helped the injured Mrs. Burleson to the floor to tend to her.

The hotel clerk escorted the woman in black to the manager's office, where he introduced her as "the lady that did the shooting." She told the manager she was tired and asked if she could sit down.

May Walker Burleson.
Courtesy of findagrave.com.

Such a scene, in such a predictably comfortable hotel in such a typically quiet downtown shopping and dining district was shocking enough. That the victim was the wife of Colonel Burleson added to the shock.

The shooter's identity was the most shocking news of all: the woman in black was Colonel Burleson's first wife, Jennie May Walker Burleson, a society daughter from Galveston, Texas, and onetime leader in the suffrage movement in Washington.

The second Mrs. Burleson was dead. The first—and, she thought, rightful—Mrs. Burleson was under arrest and charged with Isabel's murder. Getting Jennie May to confess took three days. Her trial lasted nine days. The verdict, despite her lawyers' hard-fought defense, was predictable: guilty.

While no one in the dining room at the Hotel Jefferson expected such drama along with their meat-and-three-vegetables lunch, the animosity that led to the shooting was a familiar enough backdrop: a love triangle. Jennie May Burleson saw second wife Isabel as a usurper and homewrecker. The colonel and the new Mrs. Burleson saw Jennie May as having abandoned her marriage to pursue her personal interests.

As anyone in a military family knows, the armed forces traditionally take a close interest in the personal lives of their soldiers—particularly those in leadership positions. Jennie May Burleson made sure, as her marriage deteriorated, that her husband's superiors knew the sordid details of his affairs, to a degree that hampered the colonel's career progression. For her part, she had made plenty of sacrifices for him, moving with him to his assignments in the Philippines and later in Washington, where she immersed herself in the society and politics. Her social skills did her husband credit. But she also spent months each year on archaeological digs in Oaxaca, Mexico, or staying with her mother in Texas. Her absences took more of a toll than her flamboyant 1913 horseback ride at the head of marching suffragists in Washington. Combined, her absences and his affairs culminated in a much-reported, contentious, high-priced Texas divorce. Burleson sued for the divorce, one which Jennie May fought as long as she could.

May Walker Burleson, in the center on horseback, during a March 1913 suffragists' parade along Washington's Pennsylvania Avenue. *Courtesy of Library of Congress Prints and Photographs Division.*

She hadn't wanted to lose her dashing army officer. Even more than that, she didn't want to concede her loss to the former Isabel Reece Knowlton, with whom he'd kept up a long "correspondence" and now destined to be the second Mrs. Burleson.

In convoluted proceedings, he won a divorce, but Jennie Mae's appeal had that decree set aside. Then she herself filed for divorce and won—but quickly sued to set aside that second decree. She claimed an insanity plea should have been included in both spouses' pleadings, that her lawyers had committed fraud and misrepresented her interests.

The court upheld the second divorce in March 1939. Convenient, because a year after that decree was granted in April 1937, Burleson had married Isabel in Hawaii, where he was stationed prior to their marriage.

During Jennie May's 1940 trial in Columbia, the *State* newspaper each day described her clothing to the last detail, from her "neat pumps of patent leather and satin" to her shapely, though portly, figure (which no woman would've wanted to read about herself).

The Burlesons' divorce cases had publicly aired plenty of dirty linen. The murder trial couldn't help but do the same. After a thirty-day observation at the State Hospital for the Insane and a nine-day trial, Jennie May was found guilty of voluntary manslaughter by reason of insanity. She served eight years of her twelve-year sentence, was released in October 1948 and returned to her parents' home in Galveston. She lived there until her death in 1957 at age sixty-eight. The Hotel Jefferson continued to stand on Columbia's Main Street until it was demolished in 1968.

4

THE POISONERS

A Short History of Poison

The history of poison as a murder weapon stretches far back in time. Certain poisons have had their heyday, as when the use of arsenic became so common in France for eliminating kinfolk and rivals it earned the name *poudre de succession* or "inheritance powder." In other situations, the user of the poison was more noteworthy than the poison itself. North Carolina, for instance, is home to a startling number of female serial poisoners, including well-known names such as Velma Barfield and Blanche Taylor Moore.

South Carolina cannot boast of famous dynasty poisonings or a string of murderous women—men had their turn here. The poisoning cases in the Midlands around Columbia are best defined by their unexpected quirkiness.

In 1917, Gloster Ready was sentenced in Aiken County to three years hard labor for throwing concentrated lye in J.C. Holman's well to poison him and his family. While out on bond, Ready appealed his conviction to the state's supreme court, arguing that the state hadn't proven the amount of lye used would kill anyone who drank it. That, he said, could only be proved by a chemical analysis, and the state hadn't bothered to conduct one.

The court found that lye can be diluted enough to be harmless, but testimony at trial said the water was discolored, felt slick and frothed "like soapsuds, and that it was strong enough to burn the skin." The evidence suggested the well was sufficiently contaminated. And besides, the court said, it didn't matter if the lye wasn't enough to be "poisonous, or injurious to health" or "that there may not have been enough to cause death or serious sickness." The real issue was the *intent* to poison. Ready's sentence was affirmed.

Unfortunately, neither the appellate court opinion nor the scant newspaper record explained why Ready had it in for Holman or how Holman traced the foamy soapsuds-water back to Ready's malicious hand. Sometimes, the real story is lost.

The court's decision about the lye-tainted well relied on an even older 1888 case in Abbeville where Blanche Clinkscales was charged with attempting to poison a seventeen-month-old child in her care by forcing it to drink a tincture of asafoetida. The baby didn't die, but according to the court record, the substance produced a "great and dangerous sickness."

Today, asafoetida is noted for its health benefits as an antioxidant, a digestive aid and its reputed anti-cancer properties. Used in Middle Eastern and Indian recipes, it has a pungent odor similar to garlic and is sometimes called stinking gum.

Blanche appealed her conviction, saying what she fed the baby wasn't poisonous, and besides, no one saw her administer it, so how could they say she forced it down her (which, at law, could be an assault)?

The court, after acknowledging the existence of the common law prohibitions against poisoning—which were originally brought from England to the colonies on sailing ships—held that South Carolina's criminal poisoning statute outweighed the court-made common law. According to the statute, "It is unlawful for a person to maliciously administer to, attempt to minister to…another person a poison or other destructive thing, with intent to kill that person."

The court held that forcing a child to drink a "deleterious and injurious drug" that caused "great and dangerous sickness" was the first part of the crime. The second part—and a very important part—of the crime was the intent to kill. That element was supported by a chilling bit of testimony: the defendant had heard Clinkscales warn someone, "Now, mind, one drop of this medicine will kill." Believing that only a drop could kill and then administering the drug to the baby was enough to establish intent to kill—even if the drug was not truly poisonous.

Blanche's two-year prison sentence was upheld.

Lieutenant Samuel Epes

The paper record in the murder trial of Lieutenant Sam Epes was "voluminous." And the questions about what happened continued to be difficult to answer.

Samuel and Mary Epes first met while Samuel was a student at the University of Richmond and Mary was a student at the College of William and Mary in Richmond, Virginia. They married in September 1940 and were quickly separated by the outbreak of World War II. Samuel served in an ambulance unit.

After the war, he was stationed at Fort Jackson, and the couple finally moved in together in an apartment on Sims Avenue in Columbia's Shandon neighborhood. On January 29, 1945, less than two weeks after they set up housekeeping, Samuel dropped his wife off on Main Street, where she planned to eat breakfast in Harvey's Cafeteria and do some shopping.

She wasn't home when he got back from work. Concerned, he called for help. The Columbia police "commenced a vigorous investigation and search," offering rewards and radio appeals and mailings giving her description and her known movements. By February 12, with no reports on her whereabouts, the police and the investigative officers from Fort Jackson were looking more narrowly at Samuel Epes. They'd learned he'd been shacked up with a woman in Louisiana in the months before his wife moved to join him in Columbia.

Quickly after Mary disappeared, Samuel had to be hospitalized for rabies treatments following a dog bite. He feared the authorities intended to psychoanalyze him while he was in the hospital. He wrote four letters: to his parents, Mary's parents, the provost marshal at the army base involved with the investigation and the young woman in Louisiana. He denied he'd had anything to do with Mary's "vanishing" and then proceeded to slit his wrists and throat.

He survived, and the next day—Valentine's Day—he led authorities to where he'd buried Mary on the base near Leesburg Road. He'd used one of the foxholes troops had dug for practice maneuvers; he'd added a sign saying "Latrine Closed" so no one would disturb the site.

The cold weather had preserved the body. The autopsy revealed no physical trauma, but a toxicological screening of her organs at a lab in Atlanta showed a lethal amount of Seconal Sodium, between twenty and thirty-two grains. As a comparison, the court noted that twenty grains would require ingesting thirteen capsules of the drug.

In his lengthy statement to army interrogators, Samuel admitted, "I almost went out of my mind. I visited the scene once later to try to summon courage to recover the body and give it proper burial but I couldn't and realized then for the first time what a fool I had been."

That might have been the first time he realized he was a fool but maybe not the last. He told investigators Mary had a couple of drinks and took the Seconal—normally used as a sleep aid—for menstrual cramps. He said he gave her some capsules and she took several more on her own in a space of about two hours that evening. Then he found her dead and didn't know what to do. He was afraid he would be charged with malpractice for administering drugs because he wasn't a doctor.

After he made use of the convenient foxhole, he stopped at the base dispensary to get some belladonna—another poison, derived from the deadly nightshade and used to calm the digestive track or asthma symptoms. He needed to calm his "heaving stomach."

Dr. R.P. Walton, professor of pharmacology at Medical College of South Carolina (MUSC) in Charleston, testified that taking Seconal with whiskey should have left Mary drowsy and relatively pain-free. After two more capsules, she should have been completely pain-free and tending to sleep. With additional doses, her breathing would have slowed and finally stopped.

The box of capsules found in their apartment was labeled in Lieutenant Samuel Epes's handwriting and prescribed one to two capsules for pain. He'd written his Louisiana girlfriend about his work, bragging that he routinely dispensed medicine, did minor surgeries, gave lectures and was "in command" when a doctor wasn't available. "I seem designed to be a doctor," he wrote.

Did Samuel, assigned as a "motor officer with a medical administration detachment" and with access to a dispensary of drugs, actually know that Seconal could be dangerous, even deadly?

No one other than Samuel and Mary knew what went on in that small apartment that night. Samuel said a lot, in his two written statements, but some of it was self-serving and contradictory. Only Mary's body could speak for her.

Circumstantial evidence is often criticized as weaker than direct evidence, but the appellate court cited several other courts that found circumstances often more reliable than direct evidence. One opinion said that when the circumstances point "irresistibly and exclusively" to the defendant, the evidence is surer than "the testimony of eyewitnesses, whose memory must be relied upon, and whose passions or prejudices may have influenced their testimony."

In this case, the court acknowledged that the act of poisoning a victim is rarely proven by direct evidence, such as an eyewitness, the act caught on camera or an admission of the crime. Most poisoning cases can be proven only by circumstantial evidence.

At trial, Samuel's attorney didn't want the jury to have the option of a charge less than murder, such as manslaughter. He said to the judge, "I think your Honor should charge the jury that he is either guilty of a deadly, intentional, plain, criminal murder, or that he is not guilty. Now, only by the wildest stretch of the imagination can you say that a man ought to watch his wife every time she takes a pill or every time my wife takes an anodyne."

The jury found Samuel Epes guilty of murder, with a recommendation of mercy.

In his appeal, whether he knew that Seconal could be deadly when he gave it to his wife continued to be the crux of the case. Those who thought he shouldn't have been punished so severely argued he didn't know and therefore lacked the intent needed to commit murder.

In a 1946 appellate opinion, the chief justice of the South Carolina Supreme Court argued that circumstantial evidence "must point conclusively—that is, to a moral certainty—to the guilt of the accused." He felt that Seconal was too "mild and uncertain" a drug to be relied on if the intent was to kill and that the husband's treatment of Mary's body should "have our unbounded condemnation," but "abhorrence" at what happened after death shouldn't affect the judgment about what caused the death.

The chief justice felt Samuel Epes should get a new trial for the crime of manslaughter, but unfortunately for Samuel, the chief justice's opinion was a dissent from the majority opinion. The majority upheld the guilty verdict and his sentence of life in prison.

In November 1946, over seven hundred onlookers crammed the hall of the state's House of Representatives to hear medical testimony presented to Governor Ransome Williams. (Williams also heard and denied the plea of Rose Stinnette, see chapter 4.) In that hearing, the physicians stated that Seconal was not categorized as a poison, was treated by physicians more like aspirin and that Lieutenant Epes couldn't have known of its deadly potential. After the two-hour hearing, the governor refused to overturn the jury's verdict and grant clemency.

Over a decade later, in 1959, a blue-ribbon trio of lawyers appeared before a parole board hearing on behalf of forty-one-year-old Epes: House Speaker Sol Blatt, who emphasized he was working without payment of fee or expenses; Senator J.P. "Spot" Mozingo, a successful Darlington trial lawyer; and Senator John D. Long from Union County. Preachers, a rabbi, mothers, doctors and concerned citizens spoke to the panel, which then granted Samuel Epes parole thirteen years after he carried his wife's body to a wooded area at Fort Jackson.

To the last, the question remained: Did he intend to kill her? Or was it an accident? Despite testimony from medical professionals and law enforcement officers who'd investigated the case, the answer depended on who was asking the question and what they wanted or needed to believe.

A MODERN ARSENIC POISONING

When a small town got news that a well-known and active member of the community had gone on a beach vacation and suddenly died, friends and family were understandably shocked. Seven months later, the news broke that his wife was arrested for the murder, and the puzzle of what happened in an apparently loving relationship begged to be solved.

In August 2001, Newberry native Alfred Spotts, age sixty-nine, stepped from his car in the parking lot of a Hilton Head restaurant, doubled over

The Newberry town square and old 1853 courthouse. *Courtesy of Asheville Post Card Co. and WikiProjects Postcards.*

with stomach cramps and began vomiting. He and his forty-year-old wife, Tessie Buhawe Spotts, were visiting the resort from their home in Newberry. Hilton Head was one of their favorite vacation spots.

Alfred had eaten bacon and eggs for breakfast but skipped lunch so he could enjoy a nice dinner. A former college athlete, he kept himself in good physical condition. That he would be taken ill so quickly and violently was a mystery.

The ambulance rushed him to the Hilton Head Medical Center. Two days later, on August 6, 2001, he died before doctors could find what caused his intense gastric symptoms.

When the preliminary autopsy revealed that he had ingested enough arsenic "to kill ten people," the Beaufort County Sheriff's Office, responsible for the Hilton Head area, and SLED, the state equivalent of the FBI, began investigating.

Unfortunately for poisoning victims, even medical teams at large trauma centers have trouble recognizing arsenic poisoning because the cramps, vomiting and diarrhea so insidiously and effectively mimic severe gastroenteritis or more obscure illnesses such as Guillain-Barré or cholera. Unfortunately for poisoners, arsenic is a heavy metal that never disappears and can be detected in human tissue and bones decades after exposure and death. Tests on Napoleon's hair almost one hundred years after his death showed extremely high levels of arsenic—more likely from accidental exposure to arsenic-tinted wallpaper or tonics or ointments than from homicide. Regardless of the source, the arsenic was measurable generations after his death.

The first autopsy, which revealed Alfred Spotts's cause of death, was a medical autopsy in the hospital, performed to identify disease processes. After it revealed arsenic in his system, his body was exhumed in February for a more detailed forensic autopsy. This could show when he ingested the arsenic, whether in a single large dose or spread over time. Dr. Joel Sexton agreed to do the more formal autopsy. The Newberry pathologist routinely performed autopsies for county coroners and private individuals in the years before the state began employing trained medical examiners.

In this case, he sent his results to authorities but didn't reveal his findings to the press. Meanwhile, friends and family were left with questions—and fears.

Tessie and Alfred had met a decade before his death through a matchmaking ad. He had three children from his first marriage, which had ended in divorce. Tessie married Alfred in 1992, and the couple lived in a ranch-style house in Newberry. Alfred was president of Eagle Construction Company, which specialized in highway construction, and was successful enough to be recognized as South Carolina's Small Businessman of the Year in 1986. Tessie didn't work outside the home.

Alfred had graduated from the University of South Carolina, where he majored in education and lettered in basketball and baseball—one source said he also played football. He served two years with the army in Germany. He remained an enthusiastic Carolina Gamecocks supporter and continued his personal athletic activities—even participating recently in the Senior Olympics.

In December, four months after his death, Tessie appeared in the Newberry County Probate Court to contest her husband's will. Alfred left a reported estate of $11.6 million, about $19 million today. Her attorney contended that state law entitled a wife to one-third of her husband's estate, more than the $1 million (including their house) left to her. Attorneys for Alfred's children argued that Tessie had signed a prenuptial agreement limiting her to the $1 million share of his estate.

On April 13, 2002, a *Greenville News* article opened with a tantalizing line: "Beaufort County investigators think they know what Tessie Spotts did last summer." Not long after Dr. Sexton issued his autopsy report, Beaufort County authorities arrested and charged Tessie with murder. The autopsy revealed that Alfred hadn't taken a single large dose of arsenic but, rather, suffered chronic arsenic poisoning over the four months before his August death.

Jack Swerling, one of Tessie's lawyers known for his high-profile criminal defense work, responded to the arrest: "She hasn't done anything and wouldn't do anything—she loved him."

After news of her arrest, friends of Tessie's came forward to tell reporters and law enforcement how shocked they were. At her bond hearing, the *Beaufort Gazette* reported: "Cheers went up in the back of the courtroom Monday afternoon when a circuit judge announced he would set a bond."

During the bond hearing, Solicitor Randolph Murdaugh III referred to Tessie as a "mail order bride" who "stood to gain millions upon her husband's death." From 1920 to 2005, Murdaughs had served as Fourteenth Judicial Circuit solicitor in succession, from grandfather to father to son. Twenty years after this particular hearing, the Murdaugh name became internationally recognized when Randolph's daughter-in-law and grandson were shot to death on the family hunting estate in nearby Hampton County. By the time Randolph's son Alex Murdaugh faced trials in 2023 for financial crimes and for the murders, Randolph had died, the last in that long family line of solicitors.

The Newberry Opera House. *Courtesy of Chanilim714 via Wikimedia Commons.*

In court testimony about whether to set bond, Alfred's daughter-in-law testified that Tessie was "a master of deception" and that she believed "she will kill again if she is released," that she'd always been afraid Tessie would kill Alfred, that she'd only married him for his money. In addition, Alfred's daughter said she feared for her life if Tessie was released.

But friends from Newberry also appeared at the Beaufort County bond hearing to testify to the strength of the Spottses' marriage, of their "love and devotion," how much they admired each other, how they were always together and how difficult it was to believe the charges. In addition to those who traveled to Beaufort to testify, Tessie's defense attorney presented to the court thirty letters of support from friends of the couple.

Though she had no criminal history, she was a native of the Philippines, so the prosecutor argued she could be a flight risk. Her attorneys pointed out she'd had seven months since his death and five months since she learned of the investigation if she wanted to flee the country.

Granting bond in a murder case is relatively rare because of the severity of the crime, but in this case, the judge set bond at $100,000, which would require her to post a $10,000 surety. She also had to surrender her passport and limit her travels to her home county of Newberry and to Richland and Lexington Counties to visit her lawyers' offices.

Three years later, a 2005 article in *The State* announced, "Rich wife could be tried this year in arsenic death." Duffie Stone, a deputy solicitor in Randolph Murdaugh's office, said the delays in trying the case had several causes, including a crowded criminal court docket and the complexity of the case. Solicitor Murdaugh told journalist John Monk, "Because it is circumstantial and scientific, it is an awful lot more difficult case to try than it is where you got a video of somebody shooting somebody during an armed robbery."

Sheriff Lee Foster in Newberry County told Monk, "It's still an emotional issue. There are a lot of people who support the Spotts children, and a lot who support Tessie." She was no longer living full time in Newberry. Being the talk of the town likely got old after a while.

The case remained in limbo. Five years after Alfred Spotts's death, Duffie Stone stepped into Randolph Murdaugh's position as solicitor. An article in the local paper detailed the expense of holding prisoners in the county jail awaiting trial; the rise in violent crimes; and the lack of courtroom space, solicitors and staff to bring complex cases to trial. The problem was nationwide, not limited to South Carolina. While the U.S. Constitution promises defendants the right to a speedy trial, the defendant's attorney must request a speedy trial. As Solicitor Stone pointed out, few file that motion.

In the Spotts case, the accused was not a "career criminal" and wasn't presenting a risk to the public. Stone told the *Island Packet*, "If I've got a career criminal in jail and they bond out, I know for a fact that they'd commit another crime before I prosecute them. That makes me want to speed up their trial." Tessie Spotts didn't present that risk, and she remained out on bond and continued to live her life peacefully, though still under suspicion.

Poisoning cases are difficult to prove in court. On the afternoon he died, Alfred Spotts had gone for a run and cooled off with a bottle of water—the last item he was known to have ingested. The bottle was, of course, long discarded before the autopsy reports revealed the presence of arsenic. What was the source of the arsenic? It comes in many forms and often has markers that can indicate its original source or form. Sometimes the source of arsenic can be traced—which can help the prosecution build its case. Other times, it can't be traced. And how did Alfred consume the arsenic during the four months before the final catastrophic dose? Could it have been an accidental or an environmental exposure? Those questions must be answered to meet the burden of "beyond a reasonable doubt" required in a criminal case.

In June 2009, eight years after Alfred's death, the solicitor entered a *nolle prosequi*—which translates as "not to wish to prosecute." In South Carolina, a "nol pros" means the solicitor has decided not to pursue the case. The $10,000 bond surety was returned, and the questions were not resolved.

For family and friends on both sides of this tragedy, the questions remain open and their loyalties determined by things that can't always be proven in court.

5

HEADLINE CRIMES

Pee Wee Gaskins

Donald Henry Gaskins claimed the only time he'd heard someone use his full name was in court. For his whole life, he'd been Pee Wee—slightly built, shorter than five-foot-five, described by some as intelligent and polite, by others as "the meanest man in America." Serial killers tend to want to puff up their numbers, to measure themselves against others who've made killing into a game or a contest. Some serial killers, such as Ted Bundy or Henry Lee Lucas, are known by their own names. Some have a catchy nickname awarded by the press, like the Son of Sam or the Grim Reaper. Others are recognized only by geography or some descriptive of their career: the Golden State Killer or the Texarkana Phantom or Jack the Ripper. Very few achieve the status of being mononymous, recognized immediately with only a single name. South Carolina's Pee Wee holds that status, at least in this state.

He was sent on his first trip to reform school in 1946, at age thirteen, after a girl he knew interrupted him while he was burglarizing her family's home. He attacked her with the axe she'd used to threaten him. She survived the beginning of his colorful and creepy career.

He proved adept at escaping custody, including jumping from the second story of the Florence County Courthouse during his trial for carnal knowledge of another thirteen-year-old girl. That time, he hid in the swamps for several weeks, and the story circulated that the trackers thought they had him when the hounds gathered and bayed. Pee Wee had tied the dogs together to a tree and got away.

The hearse he drove around Florence County added to his mystique. A highlight of his career, he said, was serving three years in the Atlanta federal prison, where he "studied" under members of the Genovese crime family.

Most of Pee Wee's criminal career centered on the Pee Dee region of South Carolina, near where he was born. But his most attention-getting crime happened in Columbia, inside the state's maximum-security prison in the cellblock housing the men awaiting execution in the state's electric chair.

By his own report, Pee Wee began killing steadily in 1969, when he was in his thirties. His victims shared no common traits: old, young, men, women, people he knew, victims he picked up hitchhiking, those he killed for someone else and a two-year-old and her pregnant mother. Authorities connected him with thirteen bodies, and his wild story seemed at an end after he was convicted of one murder and confessed to seven more.

In 1976, when the U.S. Supreme Court ruled the death penalty as applied by the courts was unconstitutional, he was saved from the electric chair. He was locked away for life in Columbia's Central Correctional Institution, a post–Civil War pile of bricks and razor wire looming between the Congaree River and Huger Street.

Central Prison in downtown Columbia housed death row inmates. *Courtesy of Richland Library, Columbia, South Carolina.*

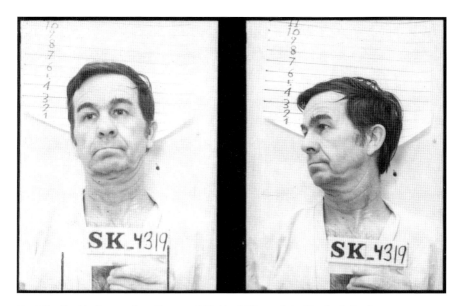

Pee Wee Gaskins's mug shot. *Courtesy of Richland Library, Columbia, South Carolina.*

Over the years, Pee Wee worked his way into the position of a trustee in the prison. He learned that fixing things—toilets, electrical outlets, plumbing, televisions or radios, whatever needed repair—let him spend more time out of his cell than he did in it. He also had a cunning about earning money and didn't waste it on vices available on the sly inside, so he always had cash when he needed to bribe an inmate or a guard. Inmates, their visitors and even guards—for enough money—always helped him get what he needed.

Pee Wee knew how to deal in favors, but he also knew how to deal in intimidation. One story had him confronting a crazy inmate who routinely threw urine on the food cart and on the trustee delivering the food. Pee Wee's solution was simple: he sprayed lighter fluid through the bars into the inmate's cell and threatened to "light him up" if they couldn't come to an understanding. The two had no more problems.

Pee Wee had a side to his personality not explained simply by cataloguing his crimes, a side that explained why others were willing to help him. Every week, Pee Wee would take that crazy inmate a Snickers bar from the canteen. He knew the man never had money for a treat. Defense attorney Grady Query quoted Pee Wee as saying, "Even crazy people can think and they can enjoy a Snickers bar."

In the old Central Prison, one row of cells backed up to another row, separated by a service hall about four feet wide where the mechanical, electrical and plumbing works ran. In 1980, Cell Block 2 housed 175 prisoners. Of the fifteen men on Death Row, only one was Black—Rudolph Tyner, a onetime drug dealer from New York convicted of murdering Bill and Myrtle Moon.

The Moons once owned and operated a coastal seafood restaurant. Later, as they got older and wanted a less demanding schedule, Bill Moon owned a little store in Murrells Inlet. By all accounts, it would've been hard to find anyone with ill words to say about the Moons, which made the events of March 1978 all the more painful and inexplicable.

Rudolph Tyner, fresh in from New York and staying at a friend's house, scoped out the store down the road and then reentered as the Moons were preparing to close for the day. He demanded the $200 in the till, ran out of the store, returned and shot both the Moons dead.

Police didn't have much trouble piecing together the story. Tyner was convicted and sent to Death Row at Central Prison.

As the Moons' son Tony Cimo endured endless hearings, then Tyner's appeal and a second trial, he became increasingly angry and frustrated at the lethargic pace of justice on behalf of his parents. The smirk on Tyner's face and the image of Cimo's mother bent over her husband's body as she was shot enraged him.

Convinced the state would never execute Tyner, Cimo began asking around, looking for a connection inside the prison who could do what needed to be done.

Eventually, Cimo made contact with Pee Wee.

After the fact, those outside found it hard to imagine that such a wild, convoluted plot could be not only hatched but also carried out in the confines of Death Row, inside a maximum-security prison.

Pee Wee was only too happy to oblige Cimo. He disliked Tyner's New York brashness. An admitted racist, he felt Tyner treated him like a servant. He told Cimo if he couldn't figure out a way to do it, he'd tell him so.

Pee Wee kept his word, but he didn't always trust that others would. Inmates could place phone calls but couldn't receive them. Pee Wee decided to tape his conversations with Cimo's representative and eventually with Cimo himself—an insurance policy for later.

Initially, the plan was to poison Tyner. Several attempts failed.

Pee Wee then decided the best option would be to blow him up. On his own tape-recorded phone call, Pee Wee can be heard asking for "however much of a stick of dynamite he could get" and a detonator. His source outside said he could obtain C-4 explosive and that would work better because it was more stable and could be shaped to fit into anything. Pee Wee asked for a "baseball-size hunk" and specified the wire rig and connectors he wanted.

Pee Wee was insistent on the best explosive for the job. "Well a guarantee don't mean much to us. We can't bring him [the supplier] over here and show him the [guy] still walkin' around and ask for our money back."

They smuggled the small components inside cigarette packets and hid the C-4 in a radio. Pee Wee's trustee status meant he could keep a toolbox and soldering iron inside his cell.

One of Pee Wee's regular visitors, introduced to him by his attorney Grady Query, was Dr. Jim Beatty, a minister and English teacher at Coastal Carolina University who began interviewing Pee Wee for a possible book. Years later, podcaster Jeff Keating interviewed Dr. Beatty about his visits and about the influence Pee Wee had inside. Beatty, who knew and respected Bill Moon, admitted he didn't realize until after Tyner's death that he had unwittingly played a part in it.

Beatty, of course, knew nothing of Pee Wee's scheme to murder Tyner, although during one visit, Pee Wee pointed out Tyner as "the man who killed your friend." As a kind man and a football fan, Beatty was happy to get a length of television wire shipped to Pee Wee, so he could hook up TVs in various cells so inmates could all watch football games.

Using his ever-present cache of money and his ability to deal, Pee Wee paid seven dollars and some candy and crackers from the canteen for a small radio with a speaker just the size he needed.

Poison had proven complicated. Blowing up his victim proved simple. Pee Wee delivered to Tyner's cell a plastic cup with a speaker in the bottom. Though Pee Wee managed to regularly visit Tyner's cell to repair his toilet and deliver drugs, he and Tyner also yelled to each other through the air vents that ran from the cells into the service hallway. With the speaker, Pee Wee said, they wouldn't have to yell. All Tyner had to do was take the two wires Pee Wee ran through the air vents, hook them onto the screws in the bottom of the cup and hold the cup up to his ear like a phone.

On September 2, 1982, when Pee Wee plugged his end of the wire into the electrical outlet, the explosion took off part of Tyner's head and his hand. He died on-site in the prison hospital.

Killing a man on Death Row, in an explosion inside a maximum-security prison on a secure cellblock, was a headline crime. Guards turned the cellblock upside down. Inside and outside, too many people knew pieces of the conspiracy and too many had reasons to help the state build the case against Pee Wee and Tony Cimo.

Experienced prosecutors Jim Anders and Richard "Dick" Harpootlian brought the case in the Richland County Courthouse. Jack Swerling, a former partner in private practice with Harpootlian and, before that, a classmate at Clemson in the late 1960s, defended Pee Wee. Swerling later defended Larry Gene Bell, who kidnapped and murdered two young women in Columbia, one of thirteen death-penalty defenses in Swerling's career (see chapter 6).

Pee Wee officially returned to Death Row after his conviction for Tyner's murder. He was executed on September 6, 1991, a man almost too small for the electric chair.

In 1983, thirty-six-year-old Cimo pleaded guilty to conspiracy and was sentenced to eight years, but he was sent to a halfway house after six months. Parole was denied at his first hearing because, as one parole board member said, he didn't think it proper to be seen as encouraging vigilantism. Cimo was paroled in 1986, after serving less than three years.

Even though he had dropped out of school and received little education, Pee Wee knew the value of telling his own story. Starting in May 1990, he dictated hundreds of hours of tapes and gave interviews to writer Wilton Earle, who transcribed and published *Final Truth* in Pee Wee's own words. He laid claim to killing over one hundred people, though most take that number with a grain of common sense. Even as he sat on Death Row, Pee Wee found that confessing to crimes could earn him day trips out of prison to visit alleged burial sites—even if the trips yielded nothing.

Home Alone

Working parents likely harbor at least some fear about their kids at home alone after school, imagining a kitchen fire or a fall or all the things a fretful mind can conjure up. On August 4, 2000, Judy Carpenter came home after work, opened the door and found something beyond a mother's wildest imaginings. Jessica, the youngest of her three daughters, was dead. She'd been murdered in her family's home, stabbed with a knife from the kitchen.

Aiken, South Carolina, is a small town. Lots of people knew the seventeen-year-old rising Aiken High School senior because she played in the band or from her part-time job greeting diners at the Red Lobster.

The town rallied in the way caring communities do: Scent dogs from the Aiken Bloodhound Tracking Team started searching. Posters with her photo, asking for leads, appeared all over town. Investigators conducted more than three hundred interviews and tested almost one hundred DNA samples through the SLED lab. In 2020, her mother told Matthew Enfinger at the *Aiken Standard*, "Not all communities would have reacted like that. In larger communities it would've been just another number in the day. They treated her with dignity and respect." Even twenty years later, her mother remembered the hard work and the kindnesses offered.

The case, however, was not quickly solved. Seldom is the public aware of how wide authorities cast their nets in an investigation. In Jessica's case, they were looking at any case in the region that might be related. One promising lead surfaced in October, two months after Jessica's murder, when Reinaldo Rivera was arrested for the rape and murder of four women and a vicious attack on another between July 1999 and September 2000. They hoped that Rivera would solve Jessica's case because having two different killers preying on young women around Aiken and Augusta at the same time was too chilling to contemplate.

Physically, Jessica resembled the victims Rivera had attacked—young, slender, long brown or blond hair. In South Carolina, seventeen-year-old Melissa Faye Dingess disappeared from Graniteville. Seventeen-year-old Tiffaney Shereese Wilson and her little two-month-old daughter Kaitlyn disappeared from a grocery store in North Augusta; Kaitlyn was found alive, abandoned in her carrier at the Georgia Welcome Center on Interstate 20. Across the state line in Georgia, eighteen-year-old Tabitha Leigh Bosdell disappeared in Augusta. The three teens had been spirited away from shopping areas or restaurants and found bound and dumped in rural areas. All had been brutally attacked and beaten. In addition, twenty-one-year-old Marni Glista, stationed at Fort Gordon, was found in her apartment; she died five days after the attack.

During that fifteen-month period, investigators began making connections, but only after eighteen-year-old Chrisilee Barton managed to survive an attack did the evidence finally point to a suspect. On October 10, 2000, a man approached Chrisilee outside the Huddle House in North Augusta, offering her work as a photographer's model. She did her best to put him off and then tried to lose him in traffic as she drove to her stepfather's apartment, but the man followed her and pushed his way into the apartment. She survived the brutal attack, but he later returned to double-check the scene. He again strangled and stabbed her in the neck to make sure she was dead.

Miraculously, Chrisilee lived. Her publicized description of her attacker prompted Reinaldo Rivera's coworker and his sister-in-law to tell police they suspected him. As police closed in, he hid in a motel room and unsuccessfully tried to kill himself by slitting his wrists.

After his arrest, and as the case to convict him proceeded toward trial, his wife, Tammy, took the unusual step of writing an open letter on behalf of her and her family to those he'd harmed:

> We want to express our deepest sympathy for all the victims and their families. We have been praying and continue to pray for the families and all that are involved....In reading about the victims I prayed to God that the person committing these horrible acts would be apprehended, not knowing it was my own husband. We believe God did not allow him to die in the motel room for at least (two) reasons; one so that the unsolved cases could be solved and two that total justice can be served....My life is shattered and I just ask that the community have compassion not so much for me but for my two small children who are victims also. We have asked God over and over Why? How could this have happened? We just do not have the answers and probably never will.

In January 2004, Rivera was tried in Georgia for the murder of army sergeant Marni Glista and for the attack on Chrisilee Barton. He attempted to turn the court proceedings into a farce, ignoring his counsel and choosing to represent himself, making a rambling statement directly to the jury and then refusing to participate in the trial, criticizing the judge and prosecutor in open court and announcing, "This is a joke. This is a circus here." He also said he was mentally ill and should be a study subject so investigators could learn from his situation.

Rivera was convicted and sentenced to death for Sergeant Glista's murder and to seven life sentences plus 105 years in prison for his other crimes in Georgia. Following the Georgia verdict, the cases in South Carolina were not tried.

Despite the horror of his crimes and the similarity that Sergeant Glista's murder had happened inside her home, Rivera's DNA didn't match that of Jessica's killer.

Investigators continued searching for killers with similar patterns of violent behavior. In 2002, investigators looked at Marc Evonitz after he was identified as Kara Robinson's kidnapper in Columbia (see chapter 3). Also in 2002, when recent college graduate Stephanie Bennett's body was found in her Raleigh, North Carolina apartment, Aiken investigators compared notes with Raleigh investigators to see if their then-unsolved cases might be related. (See *Triangle True Crime Stories*, The History Press, 2021, about the intense hunt to obtain DNA from Stephanie's killer.)

In October 2000, Reinaldo Rivera was arrested just over a week after the *CSI* series debuted on television. DNA was first used in a criminal case in England in 1989—to first exonerate one young man who'd falsely confessed to the rapes and murders and then to convict Colin Pitchfork of the crimes. The first use of DNA to free a wrongly convicted man happened in the United States that same year, releasing Gary Dotson ten years after his Chicago conviction. When *CSI* introduced DNA science on television screens in living rooms across the country, the seismic shift in forensic investigations became part of the cultural conversation.

The FBI's CODIS (Combined DNA Index System) was first implemented in 1998—three years after the United Kingdom's DNA database became operational. Getting the U.S. system operational was one hurdle. Getting local and state agencies to fill out the forms and upload their files took longer.

As a result, the system was still relatively new in 2000. DNA testing moved slowly because of the backlog of cases and the lab time required to test samples. A case where the killer seems random and unknown is the hardest kind for law enforcement to solve. Could the new technology really bring answers to the family?

Days after the second anniversary of Jessica's death, CODIS matched the DNA from her crime scene to DNA recently uploaded from an arrestee entered in the Georgia database. Investigators finally had a name: Robert Franklin Atkins.

At the time, Atkins was sitting in a state prison in Waycross, Georgia, for violating his probation after a theft conviction. Court reviews of his records showed he'd spent a considerable part of his adult life in prison, he'd lived various places in the Southeast and he'd received psychiatric treatment on occasions, including as a child.

Atkins had been working for an Airborne Express subcontractor, wearing an Airborne uniform and making deliveries in an Airborne truck the first time he stopped at the Carpenters' house in July. Trouble was, when he returned on August 4, he was on business of his own when he rang the bell and asked Jessica if he could use the phone to check on a package. After pretending to make the call, he attacked her, strangled her and cut her throat.

After his arrest, Atkins agreed to take investigators to the spot where he'd hidden the murder weapon; he'd wrapped the knife in a T-shirt and stuffed it under a brush pile near U.S. Highway 1.

Over the next four years, Atkins repeatedly changed his legal counsel, filed multiple motions and delayed the proceedings. Finally, on May 23, 2006, he pleaded guilty to first-degree criminal sexual conduct, murder, kidnapping and two lesser charges. As reported in the *Augusta Chronicle*, Judge Diane Goodstein asked him if he was sure he understood the consequences of his plea: While he would avoid the risk of a death penalty conviction, he would serve his life in prison. "Do you understand that you will spend the remainder of your life behind bars? Out feet first, in a box." He was sentenced to two consecutive life sentences.

In a civil lawsuit, Jessica's father sued Airborne, its subcontractor and insurers on behalf of her estate, claiming the company was negligent in hiring Atkins without conducting a criminal background check. At the time he was hired, a check of his record would have shown felony convictions for burglary and weapons charges. The South Carolina Appellate Court held that Atkins's intentional criminal actions were not covered as work events by the company's insurance policy; any settlement or other resolution of the lawsuit did not appear in news reports.

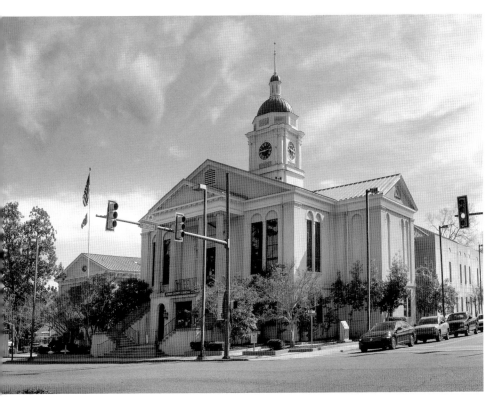

The Aiken County Courthouse and downtown square. *Courtesy of Andy Hunter.*

As the years following Jessica's death passed into decades, her family and the community continued to remember her—planting a memorial magnolia tree, establishing a memorial garden near where her mother worked and endowing a scholarship in her name at the University of South Carolina–Aiken. Judy continued to talk about her daughter, wanting people to remember her and her story, to warn others that predators exist and to remind herself and others what a bubbly young woman Jessica was.

A Terrifying Summer

Reading headlines on yellowing newsprint and studying the grainy black-and-white photos can't capture the frisson of fear that swept Columbia during the summer of 1985. With unexpected force, families—especially those with children—were swept into the reality that tragedy could happen in their own front yards. For twenty-eight days, starting on May 31, those living in and around Columbia knew that the worst could happen to their children. And even when the boogeyman finally had a face and a name and was locked away, their world was still different.

The story has been recounted in books, articles, television documentaries, a made-for-TV movie and on the stage at the Miss America pageant. The wave of fear started at the end of a long driveway in Lexington County where seventeen-year-old Shari Faye Smith stopped at the mailbox. She was on her way home from an end-of-the-school-year pool party. Her dad saw her car down at the road. When she didn't come to the house in a few minutes, he went to check on her.

The driver's door was open, her purse on the front seat. Her medication for her rare form of diabetes was there. She never went anywhere without it. The car was running. Mail was scattered on the ground. But Shari was gone. He looked around in the shrubs and along the road, in case she'd had a spell. He called her name. Then he ran for the phone.

Such an ordinary routine. His daughter coming home in the middle of the afternoon from a party with her friends. A stop at the mailbox. Then the cold stab of panic. The Smith family, strong in their faith and active in their community, worked with the police. Their friends and church members gathered around offering support, searching for Shari. Three days later, the Smiths' phone rang at 2:30 in the morning. The man, whose voice sounded electronically distorted, apologized for taking her and said they'd get a letter soon.

Police didn't wait for the post office in Lexington to open. The postmaster helped them search the bags for the letter addressed to the Smiths. Inside, the two-page Last Will and Testament handwritten by Shari said she wanted a closed casket. "I'll be with my Father now. Please do not become hard or upset. Everything works out for the good for those that love the Lord."

After the phone call, the Lexington County sheriff asked the FBI for its expertise. John Douglas, one of the founding profilers in the FBI's Behavioral Analysis Unit, developed a psychological portrait of the killer—someone who'd committed sexual assault and maybe kidnapping in the past, who had some criminal experience. Someone who had trouble maintaining relationships and perhaps had experience in electronics. As with most profiles, that information might tell them they had the right guy—but only after they found him.

The taunting, cruel, creepy phone calls to the family continued, and the FBI recorded them. Douglas suggested using Shari's older sister Dawn, a college student in North Carolina, to lure him into talking longer. They traced the calls but always arrived at a pay phone in an isolated area to find the receiver dangling and the area clean of prints.

The investigation operated with the ever-present fear that he'd harm someone else. The fear became reality on June 14. In neighboring Richland County, nine-year-old Debra May Helmick was snatched from her front yard. She was playing with her brother. Her dad was inside their trailer. A neighbor across the road saw a car drive past and turn around. The driver stopped, grabbed Debra May around the waist and stuffed her in the car as she kicked and screamed. The neighbor was too far away to get more than one letter of the license tag.

The Smith family continued getting the same excruciating phone calls. A few days later, a call gave directions to Debra May's body.

Shari's handwritten letter to her parents gave investigators their best physical clue; forensic specialists at SLED used electrostatic detection equipment to reveal a partial phone number indented into the paper. Someone had written the number on the legal pad, on the sheet affixed on top of the page Shari later used. The phone number led them to a married couple—clearly not matches to Douglas's profile of the killer. But the couple recognized the voice from a recorded phone call: "That's Larry Gene Bell." He worked for their electrical business and house-sat for them while they were visiting family. The legal pad came from their house.

Larry Gene Bell was arrested on June 27, 1985, the day after Debra May Helmick's funeral.

He matched the FBI profile. The thirty-six-year-old had been arrested for incidents of assault and battery and for attempted kidnapping in the mid-1970s. He was older than the profiler expected, but his past gave him the criminal sophistication these crimes suggested he would have. In addition to his earlier arrests, he was also suspected in the disappearances of several young women in Charlotte, though nothing was ever confirmed and he admitted nothing. (See *Charlotte True Crime Stories*, The History Press, 2019.)

Attorney Jack Swerling, veteran of many criminal defenses, represented Larry Gene Bell at his 1986 trial. To the jury, Bell's outbursts and disruptions during the trial and his testimony on the witness stand looked more like manipulation than insanity. He was found guilty of kidnapping and murdering Shari and sentenced to death.

The following year, he was tried, convicted and sentenced to death for Debra May Helmick's kidnapping and murder. He chose the electric chair rather than lethal injection and died on October 4, 1996.

The boogeyman never admitted his crimes. The closest he came was telling John Douglas, "All I know, is that the good Larry Gene Bell couldn't have done this, but the bad Larry Gene Bell could have." In an interview with A&E, John Douglas said, "I hope I never see another one like that again."

Shari's father, Bob Smith, served as chaplain for the sheriff's department. Dawn became Miss South Carolina and second runner-up in the Miss America pageant; as a singer/songwriter and inspirational speaker, she continued to share the story of the little sister who looked so much like her and how they loved to sing together.

6

THE GAMBLERS

Singer Kenny Roger's hit song "The Gambler" offered good advice about how to play your cards—advice apparently much needed but little heeded by some gamblers. As a couple of South Carolina cases illustrate, knowing when to hold and when to fold can be difficult for a true gambler to discern.

"I'M GOING TO DISNEY WORLD!"

Does the city exist that hasn't, at some point, faced a political scandal? For 1970s Columbia, the scandal involved corruption within its 250-member police department. City leaders vowed to clean it up and went looking outside the state to find a police chief to help repair the image and the integrity of the department. They found Arthur Hess just outside of Chicago, where he'd served as police chief for seven years in two separate suburban departments—Downers Grove and Northfield. In his almost two decades in law enforcement, Hess was known as a solid, progressive manager—or as John O'Brien reported in the *Chicago Tribune*, "his specialty was administration, not chasing street criminals." His lawyer later described him as "a bright and honest police executive, but he was a terrible investigator." That distinction was subtle but later became important.

Hess arrived in Columbia to take office in 1978. By 1981, he was facing his own scandal, accused of soliciting bribes from a gaming machine operator.

The case was only a hint of the video poker machine battles that would rage within the state over the next two decades. A largely unregulated industry, the machines gradually became a flashpoint between those making money on machines in convenience stores dotted around the state and those who heard stories of a neighbor stopping to buy a loaf of bread and losing a week's pay in a machine—or a house or a child's college fund. According to a study reported in the *New York Times*, video poker was "the crack cocaine of gambling"—cheap, easy to stumble across while running an errand and deceptively addictive. The *Times* article reported that South Carolina hosted the "country's largest video gambling industry," with its 34,000 machines and estimated $2.8 billion annual revenue.

In 1999, after public outcry and legislative wrangling, a South Carolina Supreme Court ruling brought video poker to a quick end. The court decreed a deadline on June 30, 2000, when all the machines in the state had to be unplugged.

As Chief Hess took office in 1998, the gambling business had just begun to soak deep into the fabric of the state. Dealing with video poker wasn't his main mandate. He'd been hired because some Columbia officers were allegedly doing favors for area bootleggers and manufacturing evidence in some drug cases. But three years after his arrival, Hess surprised Columbia residents and officials. He was on trial for bribery and extortion, obstruction of justice (for passing information about a drug investigation to a possible target) and for misconduct in office.

Hess's time in Columbia began to unravel when Joel Hendrix went to the state's attorney general claiming Hess had solicited a bribe from him. Hendrix, owner of a gaming machine company that supplied video games, pinball and pool tables to area businesses, said Hess offered to advise him on how to stay out of jail for the low cost of $1,000 a month.

The attorney general and SLED agents were parked at a rest stop on Interstate 26 in Calhoun County when Hendrix, wired with a microphone, met Hess for the second time. The evidence of the first meeting was Hendrix's word against Hess's since it wasn't taped. The second meeting recorded the details clearly enough to present to a future jury.

Later, according to court documents, Hess would claim he suspected Hendrix was "a major local crime figure," so he was conducting a one-man undercover sting operation. Hess told no one within the Columbia Police Department and no law enforcement officials in any of the other counties involved because he feared corruption and leaks. Despite plenty of criticism from those who believed Hess was innocent, investigators

Above: The Lexington County Courthouse. *Courtesy of Ralph Hightower via Wikimedia Commons.*

Left: The Calhoun County Courthouse. *Courtesy of Bill Fitzpatrick via Wikimedia Commons.*

didn't buy that version of the story—and at least in part, neither did the juries.

The convoluted case involved two state trials—one in Lexington County and one in Calhoun County. In both, Hess was convicted of misconduct in office. In the second trial, in Calhoun, he was also convicted of obstruction of justice. Neither jury found the evidence of bribery and extortion convincing beyond a reasonable doubt and acquitted him on those charges.

Sentenced to three years, Hess was released from jail on bond and started working at a local real estate sales office while his attorneys appealed his conviction.

On June 7, 1985, the case took a bizarre turn. Hess's car—with bloodstains matching his blood type inside—was found abandoned in a grocery store lot a few miles from his Columbia home. Had his past as a law officer caught up with him? Had he been involved in the kind of corruption that can lead to serious consequences? Or had he gone on the run to avoid serving a prison sentence?

Ten days later, a car owned by Mary McEachern was found abandoned off Interstate 20 in Augusta, Georgia, about seventy-five miles from Columbia. The interior was also bloodstained. McEachern and Hess had worked together at the real estate office.

Authorities suspected the bloodstained cars had been staged to suggest foul play. They didn't ignore the possibility the couple had been harmed, but they were also searching for a very-much-alive Arthur Hess and his girlfriend.

Two months later, Hess's wife was in court as her husband's criminal defense lawyer stepped in to protect her home from forfeiture. The family residence had been used to secure Hess's $10,000 bond; his failure to appear in court meant authorities could revoke the bond and seize her house. After her husband's legal troubles began, Mrs. Hess had returned to work as a nurse to support her family. She had no idea where her husband was or what happened. Out of consideration for her and her three children, the judge postponed his ruling on the forfeiture.

Seven months later, on January 26, 1986, vacationers from Columbia spotted Hess and McEachern standing in line waiting to board Spaceship Earth at Disney World's Epcot Center. Disney World security contacted the FBI, which took the two into custody until they could be transported back to Columbia.

Richland County prosecutor Jim Anders told the *New York Times*, "He should have gone to Yellow Knife in the Yukon, not the Magic Kingdom."

When first questioned in Florida, the couple presented valid drivers' licenses in assumed names, but fingerprints confirmed their identities as Hess and McEachern. The couple had been living in Tampa in inexpensive lodging and managing a mobile home park. Their neighbors and coworkers had nice things to say about them and were surprised by the news.

In Hess's federal appeal, the court reversed one of his misconduct convictions because being tried in both Lexington and Calhoun Counties for the same crime violated his constitutional double jeopardy protections. The court cited a U.S. Supreme Court case, saying, "At its most basic, the Double Jeopardy Clause provides three related guarantees for criminal defendants: 'It protects against a second prosecution for the same offense after acquittal. It protects against a second prosecution for the same offense after conviction. And it protects against multiple punishments for the same offense.'"

Neither jury convicted Hess on the more severe charges of bribery and extortion. Public debate continued about whether he was really conducting his own private sting operation—hinting at his lawyer's claim that Hess was a "terrible investigator."

Back in a South Carolina court, Hess apologized for running. "My action was not one of defiance in the least, but of desperation." In the end, he was given a five-year suspended sentence and five years' probation for contempt of court for fleeing the jurisdiction while on bond. The penalty could have been much stiffer: as much as five years in prison and a $25,000 fine. He also had to serve his three-year federal sentence and complete three hundred hours of community service while on probation. Mary McEachern was ordered to pay a $10,000 fine for helping him disappear.

Thirty years later, veteran WIS-TV reporter Jack Kuenzie wrote about the day he and photographer Bob Pollack were sent to Florida to interview the FBI agent who'd arrested the couple during their Disney adventure. Keunzie said he and a cameraman were listening to a radio broadcast of the nearby Challenger space shuttle launch, and he started snapping photos of the shuttle's vapor trail with a 35mm camera. He'd seen the white trail split in two but thought that must be normal.

Before their interview could begin, the agent was called away. The *Challenger* had exploded. That event has stayed in the public memory far longer than the tales of police corruption and the chief who ran away to Disney World.

Gambling Debts and Deaths

Friday the thirteenth can be an unlucky day. On the afternoon of April 13, 2012, Brett Parker sounded like he was crying when he called 911 from his spacious home in a quiet neighborhood outside Irmo.

"Who shot your wife?" the operator calmly asked.

"My friend, Bryan."

Rarely is video available of 911 callers, but home security cameras captured Brett Parker pacing around the paved area outside his garage in obvious distress, for a time even lying on his back as he talked to the operator.

Brett, a successful medical supply salesman, said he was on the toilet in the downstairs bathroom when his longtime friend and business associate Bryan Capnerhurst arrived at the home. The two had scheduled a meeting. Brett called out to Bryan that he'd join him in a minute, to go on upstairs to the office.

Within moments, Brett said, he heard gunshots. He ran up the stairs, where Bryan Capnerhurst pointed a gun at him and ordered him to open the safe. As Brett moved toward the safe in an attic alcove, he saw his wife, Tammy Parker, on the floor of their home office, her head in the bathroom, her legs still in the office. She wasn't moving.

Brett told officers that he remembered the gun he kept stashed near the safe. He grabbed it and, before Bryan could react, shot him. He checked on his wife, who appeared dead. Then he called 911.

When officers arrived, they found Bryan Capnerhurst lying in the upstairs alcove near the safe. He had in his hand the gun later determined to be the gun that killed Tammy Parker.

The Parkers were both successful in sales, but Tammy was the breadwinner. She was a statuesque blonde, energetic and engaging, and her job in pharmaceutical sales provided a comfortable income and time to spend with their two children and to sing with a local band, Jumpstart. Brett had been a standout high school athlete, playing several sports and excelling at baseball. He continued to play adult league softball. The couple was attractive, sociable and successful. Those who knew them had trouble piecing together how this could have happened.

Initially, the scene matched Brett's account—that Capnerhurst, anxious to get the money he was owed, decided to enter the house and rob the Parkers' safe. He hadn't expected to find Tammy at home and killed her. Brett shot him in self-defense.

Sign announcing Irmo's Okra Strut festival. *Courtesy of Dr. Blazer via Wikimedia Commons.*

But Sheriff Leon Lott and his investigators were thorough, and little oddities and inconsistencies soon became evident. A female crime scene investigator noted something that male investigators might have missed: if Brett Parker had been sitting on the toilet in the downstairs powder room, why wasn't the seat down?

The autopsy revealed another improbability in Brett's version of events. Bryan lay where he'd fallen, on top of cracked plastic storage boxes, with a 9mm pistol in his left hand. The medical examiner testified that the first shot to the chest killed Bryan. The second shot from Brett's .410 hit his left forearm. With that type of injury, the medical examiner said "no way" Bryan could hold the pistol and collapse with it still in his hand. He would have no control over the muscles in his hand. On cross-examination, Brett's defense attorney didn't gain any ground with questions about cadaveric spasm or a "death grip." The most likely explanation of the scene was that Brett put the 9mm pistol that killed Tammy in Bryan's hand after he died.

The time-stamped home surveillance video clearly showed Bryan Capnerhurst arriving and backing his car into a spot near the basketball goal opposite the garage. He carried a gym bag slung over his shoulder and looked relaxed and unhurried. He arrived at 12:31 p.m., but the 911 call wasn't made until 12:42 p.m.—eleven minutes later. Given Brett's account, events inside the house wouldn't have taken that long.

A crime scene photo showed Bryan's unzipped gym bag sitting on the floor upstairs. Clearly visible on top of gym clothes and shoes sat an empty gun magazine and a box of ammo. Wouldn't such heavy items have shifted to the bottom of the bag? Why would he have pulled out a box of ammunition? Wouldn't he have loaded the gun before he entered the house?

Brett had no blood on him and no sign that he'd tried to check on or revive his wife. Why had he gone outside to call 911?

Brett admitted to the initial investigator that he had a side business. He was quick to tell him—quietly, off to the side—that he was a bookie. Bryan had worked for him in that business.

Bookies aren't unheard of in small towns. Law enforcement sometimes lets the business operate because, that way, they knew who is involved. That reduced the likelihood of some dangerous, unpredictable element coming in to fill the void. And Brett Parker and his cohorts, they learned, were known as gentlemen bookies.

Bryan Capnerhurst knew Brett Parker because he'd once placed bets with him, but Bryan had given up gambling his own money. He then started working for Brett, some said as a partner or as what another bookie called a clerk, coming to Brett's home office on betting days to answer one of the two dedicated toll-free lines and record the bets—which client, which games, what amounts.

Bryan earned a percentage of the take, though the amount of his percentage wasn't publicized. According to reporter Noelle Phillips, investigators discovered that Brett owed Bryan $21,300—from 2011 football bets and from 2012 baseball bets. Bryan had been pushing him for repayment on the long-overdue debt, but Brett was having trouble coming up with the cash.

Later testimony established that Bryan no longer trusted Brett. Before he left to meet at Brett's house, he told his wife and a friend that if he wasn't out of the Parkers' house in an hour, they should call 911. However, when Bryan learned that Tammy would also be home, he felt confident he wouldn't need their backup.

Brett hadn't hesitated to tell investigators about his bookie business, but he wasn't quick to admit he'd been having an extramarital affair. In fact, he lied when asked about it. But his text messages soon provided investigators with the evidence.

Added to the pressure of Brett's debt to Bryan, his paramour testified that he wanted to leave his wife, but their finances made that difficult. Tammy also had almost $1 million in retirement investments and life insurance.

The heaviest pressure weighing on Brett Parker took a little longer to uncover. He not only took bets but also made bets—a mistake wise bookies avoid. After all, they know the odds. They know they fix those odds so "the house" wins the majority of bets, not the gambler. But Brett owed a lot of money to another Midlands bookie, Lanny Gunter. He'd known Lanny a long time. Lanny had loaned Brett $5,000 to start his own bookie business. Brett was making payments to Lanny of $5,000 to $10,000 each month to keep his gambling account current. As Noelle Phillips reported in *Gaming News*, the $176,000 debt was sizeable, but Lanny had reliable cash flow from Brett as he paid off the debt and likely wasn't pressuring him.

The evidence accumulated, and three months after the deaths, investigators charged Brett Parker with the double murders.

In May 2013, Brett Parker was tried for the two homicides in a three-week trial. After three hours of deliberation, the jury convicted him in both deaths and he was sentenced to life without parole.

The double murder was more than a domestic tragedy in quiet, suburban Irmo—it opened the thriving illegal gambling business in central South Carolina to public and law enforcement scrutiny. Early in the investigation into the deaths of Tammy and Bryan, someone anonymously dropped off a list of area bookies at the Irmo Police Department. Even though sports betting is illegal in South Carolina, those looking to place bets can usually find someone who knows someone who'll take a wager, especially on football

Williams-Brice Stadium at the University of South Carolina in Columbia. *Courtesy of IdibriConsulting via Wikimedia Commons.*

and basketball games. Most bookies keep a low profile and take clients only on referral from people they know. After all, it's not like they can advertise on bus benches or Craigslist. Bookie and bettor tend to maintain their relationship over time.

That anonymously delivered list led investigators to a group of bookies, most of whom had operated in the Midlands for years. Bookies tend to know each other. When one finds his betting book too lopsided for comfort, putting him at risk of paying out more money than he's taking in, he'll "lay off" some of his bets with another bookie in order to spread the risk—not unlike how insurance companies will pool risks with other insurance companies.

With the list of local bookies in hand, the U.S. Secret Service and the Richland County Sheriff's Office began unraveling the region's web of gambling operations. State and federal prosecutions followed. Caught in that net was Jack Parker, Brett's father and mentor in the business. Reports say Jack Parker once ran a video poker machine business, placing the machines in convenience stores and other small businesses around the state. When the state legislature and the courts shut down that operation, Jack Parker went to work for Lanny Gunter as a bookie. Brett was in business with his father until he set up his own operation.

As a result of the murders, state and federal authorities unwound the skein of relationships among bookies operating in the Midlands. After a legal debate over whether their operation made enough money and had the requisite five or more participants to meet the threshold for federal action, Jack Parker and his business partner, Doug Taylor, were convicted of operating an illegal gambling ring. The prosecutors called them "long-term, lifetime bookies." Lanny Gunter and two others testified in the trial; they had already been convicted on federal gambling charges. Gunter served a short sentence; the other two defendants, as well as Jack Parker and Doug Taylor, were granted probation rather than prison time.

7

THE TRICKSTERS

TERROR CLOSE TO HOME

To hear the words "domestic terrorists" brings to mind the smoking, ragged remains of the Oklahoma City Federal Building or the five-year-long hunt for bomber Eric Rudolph in the North Carolina mountains or the almost twenty-year reign of Unabomber Ted Kaczynski. What likely wouldn't come to mind is the older couple who moved into a bungalow down the street in your small hometown or the customer who visits your business. Terrorists are odd and live elsewhere. They couldn't live in a house on a well-traveled road or be standing behind you at the grocery checkout line.

At least, that's what folks in Abbeville and Sumter likely thought.

Steven Bixby left New Hampshire in the mid-1990s and moved to Abbeville. In his late twenties or early thirties, he quickly became known around town for his impassioned talk about constitutional rights and government encroachment. After a few drinks in the local bar, he was known to punctuate his diatribes by bellowing, "Live free or die!" It was his personal motto, apparently—as well as that of his home state of New Hampshire.

A few years later, in 2000, his parents joined him in Abbeville. Plenty of South Carolina residents have neighbors who've moved from up north, looking for warmer weather or more affordable housing or less congestion. And often, family members follow them, after receiving taunting reports of a seventy-degree day while those back home are shoveling snow.

But those who knew the Bixbys in Abbeville probably didn't know they hadn't come south for the climate. New Hampshire officials held a warrant for Steven Bixby's arrest for parole violations on drunk driving and driving without a license convictions. His parents, Rita and Arthur, were facing foreclosure back home because they refused to pay taxes on their house. Rita, named the "family's constitutional mastermind," appeared to be the one who stirred up most of the trouble. The family, according to reports, had "terrorized neighbors and public officials since the 1970s with sham lawsuits, common-law tax protests and the occasional armed threat." Even the police chief in New Hampshire dreaded the visits he had to make to their house to serve legal papers.

To journalist Bob Moser, one Abbeville neighbor said he didn't give much thought to their antigovernment pamphlets and letter-writing and suing people in New Hampshire. "I just thought it was old people being grumpy. A lot of people, you think they're weird, but you wouldn't think they'd kill somebody." But Arthur and his fiery wife and son were known to unleash their anger and racial epithets. Maybe the Bixbys moved to Abbeville expecting to find a town full of like-minded people. They didn't.

Steven lived in an apartment complex. One of his neighbors told Moser, "When I first met him, I thought, 'Well, he's just a Northerner and he needs lots of prayer.'" She'd seen his temper and been on the receiving end of his threats.

Rita and Arthur bought a small white house on Highway 72, a busy road that runs from Athens, Georgia, east through Abbeville and across the state to Greenwood, Clinton and Rock Hill.

The boarded-up Bixby house sits to the right of Highway 72 outside Abbeville. *Image from Google Image capture: June 2014 © 2023 Google.*

The state highway department was widening Highway 72, right past the Bixbys' house. On December 6, 2003, state employees started staking out the construction area along the Bixby property and came to the house with maps and documents to explain the work. The Bixbys' rage went into high gear. They told anyone who would listen—verbally and in letters to state officials and the governor—that the documents produced by the state were "manufactured lies," that they had always been ready to defend their private property and, Rita said repeatedly, if anyone trespassed, "there would be hell to pay."

The highway department employees were concerned enough about the threats that they went to the sheriff's office. The state inspector said Rita was "most definitely" in charge, telling the visitors the family had plenty of guns and that trespassers would be shot.

On December 5, the inspector telephoned the Bixbys to explain what gave the state the right to come onto their property. A previous owner had signed a right-of-way easement in 1960, long before the Bixbys bought the property. Perhaps a point in the Bixbys' favor, the easement was recorded with the state highway department in Columbia, as provided in state statute, and was not recorded with the Abbeville Clerk of Court when they bought their property in 2000. That was how highway rights-of-way were handled. While it might make sense to the SCDOT and others, to someone with an entrenched suspicion of government agents, this "hidden" right-of-way easement allegedly negotiated forty years before they bought their property would sound fishy.

Rita wouldn't let the inspector talk to Arthur on the phone. She cussed and raged and threatened, then told them to come to the house and show her the papers. Even after the SCDOT officials agreed to come to the house to talk, Rita said, "Anything you got is lies." She said whatever documents they claimed to have were forgeries, that deputies had no authority over them and the family "would fight till the last breath and there would be hell to pay."

One state employee who'd already had a confrontation with the family refused to go, but three other state employees drove to the house on December 5. The screaming and fingers in the face and threats lasted about an hour as they stood in the rain.

An important element was often lost in the uproar, but according to journalist Moser, the road-widening project would take only a small corner of the Bixbys' yard. In exchange, they could buy another portion made available from the shift in the road for only one dollar. But the notion of

The Abbeville County courthouse. *Courtesy of Brian Scott via Wikimedia Commons.*

state intrusion was what ignited the Bixbys, not concepts of fair exchange or reason.

The next day, Steven told those attending a party at his former girlfriend's house that his family had another meeting about the property dispute scheduled the next day. According to court testimony, he said, "Tomorrow is the day" and "we have the guns loaded" and "when the shooting starts I will come out alive." He said the family had been planning this for a long time. The sheriff's office received calls from some who heard Steven's threats at that Sunday gathering.

On Monday, December 8, Deputy Danny Wilson drove to the Bixbys' house. As he approached the door, Steven Bixby fired a 7mm Magnum—intended for large-game hunting—through the glass in the front door, killing Wilson. Steven dragged the body inside the house and waited.

When sixty-three-year-old Constable Donnie Ouzts came to the house, he could see Deputy Wilson's car parked in front. Minutes later, Ouzts was shot in the back as he got out of his car, and he later died at the hospital. Those shots began a twelve-hour armed standoff, with officers and the Bixby men exchanging hundreds of gunshots. Later photos showed the interior of the house riddled with bullets from the firefight.

Rita was at Steven's apartment, where she'd taken their other son to keep him safe. After the first death, Steven called to tell her that "the trouble had started." Her apparent role was to notify state officials—including the governor and attorney general. According to testimony, she refused to act as an intermediary in the standoff between officers and her family. "Why would I want to help you? I wanted to be inside with them today." And she let authorities know she had enough ammunition with her to do some serious damage.

Officers quickly mobilized, and dozens surrounded the house, aided by SLED's SWAT team, a helicopter and an armored vehicle. When a state hostage negotiator failed to get any response from Steven or Arthur, officers rammed the front of the house with the armored truck and sent a bomb squad robot inside to see whether Deputy Wilson was still alive. The firefight continued for a time before Steven surrendered. Arthur was injured.

Late in the day, Rita was coaxed from Steven's apartment. She was charged with misprision of a felony (knowing about a felony and actively hiding it or lying about it to authorities), criminal conspiracy and accessory before the fact of murder. In a pretrial decision, the state supreme court held that she couldn't be eligible for the death penalty since she wasn't charged with murder.

Steven's four-day trial began on Valentine's Day 2007. He was found guilty and sentenced to death. In Rita's October 2007 trial, the seventy-five-year-old was found guilty of conspiracy and being an accessory to the murders and received a life sentence. Arthur was adjudged incompetent to stand trial and was admitted to a mental hospital.

Part of Steven's legal appeal of his conviction was that the trial judge had refused to let a title abstract researcher testify that, in searching the Bixby's property title, he found no right-of-way easement registered with the Abbeville Clerk of Court. The appellate court held that the judge correctly blocked the testimony because saying that information couldn't be found at the clerk's office and suggesting that it was "missing" would mislead the jury.

In September 2011, seventy-nine-year-old Rita Bixby died in prison. Her husband, age eighty-two, had died one week earlier. Their forty-four-year-old son was on Death Row at a prison outside Columbia.

Unfortunately, the violence sparked by the Bixbys' anger and distrust of the government was not an isolated incident. A 2003 report by the Anti-Defamation League pointed to armed confrontations between law enforcement and those calling themselves sovereign citizens in Michigan, Arizona, Texas, Missouri, Washington, Alaska, Louisiana, Tennessee, Nevada, Massachusetts and Montana. Others motivated by the movement include Timothy McVeigh and Terry Nichols, responsible for the Oklahoma

City federal building explosion—the largest act of U.S. domestic terrorism, with 168 deaths.

The sovereign citizen movement isn't easily defined or neatly categorized. Most adherents engage solely in "paper terrorism," using fake legal documents, license tags and drivers' licenses because properly registering would acknowledge the authority of state or federal governments. Some sovereign citizens file flurries of lawsuits against local political officials, judges and prosecutors and create fake checks or other transaction documents—in short, whatever can get them out of paying bills or clog up the legal or financial system in order to deny the legitimacy of the government. These actions crowd court dockets and cost taxpayers.

The current incarnation of the movement started with the Posse Comitatus, a white supremacist movement in the 1970s. They were primarily tax protestors. From their white supremacy ideology developed an unexpected off-shoot: the Moorish Nation or Moors, who hold that federal law doesn't apply to Black people. Moors contend that their ancestors were the original inhabitants of America and are due special privileges as sovereigns. They too protest the payment of taxes or the recognition of formal legal documents. The Moors have added a new wrinkle: they insist they have the right to occupy any house they like, and they often take possession of houses left abandoned, for instance, in mortgage foreclosure actions or after the death of the owners.

Some sovereign citizens make money by teaching seminars or selling literature about the movement. Others indoctrinate through online YouTube videos. Some work within the prison system recruiting members. Others offer prisoners a get-out-of-jail (but not for free) scheme with "redemption" or "accepted for value" deals to set them free—one scheme offered that hollow promise for the low fee of $4,000.

None of the various elements of the movement have an organized hierarchy. Most members loosely affiliate with family or friends or are lone operators, but no national organization or leader exists.

Some rally around Second Amendment gun ownership rights and encourage people not to register their guns. Some espouse racist white identity. Many are tax protestors. Most haven't resorted to violence. An article in the FBI's *Law Enforcement Bulletin* admits that the groups could be dismissed as a nuisance, that some of "their actions, although quirky, are not crimes" or are minor offenses. But law enforcement can't ignore the more severe financial scams, threats to judges and law officers or armed confrontations. The FBI has identified the movement as a terrorist threat.

Bob Moser, writing about the Bixbys' case for the Southern Poverty Law Center, said sovereign citizens or tax protestors or "whatever you call them, they're a hearty species that has thrived like kudzu in the piney hills" of South Carolina. According to Moser and others who keep tabs, "There may be more antigovernment extremists in the vicinity of Abbeville than anywhere else in America, with the possible exceptions of the Idaho panhandle and the Ozarks."

But white citizens aren't the only ones who put their complaints against the government into violent action—in South Carolina and elsewhere. On a Saturday afternoon in August 2018, Demetrius Alexander Brown walked into a car shop on South Pike Road East, a frontage road in Sumter off U.S. Highway 378, the Myrtle Beach Highway.

Witnesses said Brown had words with thirty-four-year-old Sharmine Pack. Some said the two men knew each other and were in a dispute over a car Brown had bought from Pack. Brown pulled a gun and shot Pack. When his victim fell, Brown walked over and shot him several times as he lay on the floor to make sure he wouldn't survive. Pack died at the local hospital.

Brown raced away in his car and was seen north of Atlanta on Monday.

Sumter law enforcement had arrested Brown before, on charges of burglary, financial fraud and domestic violence. They alerted law enforcement agencies that he identified himself as a Moorish sovereign citizen. Though officials didn't know what, if anything, that had to do with this shooting, officers knew that other Moorish sovereigns had recently resorted to violence when confronted by police in Baton Rouge and Orlando.

Marshals captured Brown four days after the shooting in Jacksonville, Florida. While he awaited trial in the Sumter County Detention Center, in true sovereign citizen fashion, he filed a sixty-four-page civil complaint asserting violation of his civil rights by thirty-one defendants, including the sheriff and other officials. In response, the federal magistrate judge returned a "detailed nine-page proper form order identifying and explaining the numerous deficiencies" in his complaint and explaining that nothing more could happen until the plaintiff corrected his document. The court dismissed the complaint.

Brown also sued, claiming he was unconstitutionally arrested and, as a result, had "suffered emotional distress, mental anguish, loss of liberty and 'other grievous injuries.'" He asked for both actual and punitive damages. In a seven-page opinion, the court dismissed that claim.

On February 19, 2022, fifteen years to the day after Steven Bixby was convicted, a jury returned on a Sunday evening and convicted Demetrius Brown.

Less than three months after his conviction, he filed suit against Sumter County's court and solicitor's office, the state of South Carolina and the state's supreme court, in motions filed *pro se* (representing himself without a lawyer). He wanted his civil motion protesting the conditions of confinement heard, some of his state convictions expunged and his record corrected with the Department of Motor Vehicles. The federal court dismissed that complaint because he "failed to state a claim upon which relief could be granted."

Brown filed other suits, before and after the murder, with the same result—and each filing meant time spent by state and federal judges and court personnel to make sure the complaints were properly reviewed.

The cases of the Bixby family and Demetrius Brown illustrate the continuum of challenges presented by those involved in the sovereign citizen movement. As the FBI observed, the cases may seem quirky—but they can also be costly, time-consuming and, in the worst case, deadly for those employed to carry out the business of state and local government.

INSURANCE FRAUD

North and slightly east of North Augusta, South Carolina, sits the home of one of the three largest settlements of a group known as Irish Travellers. Their DNA proves they are Irish, not Romani, so don't call them "gypsies." Other groups of English Travellers and Scottish Travellers with similar histories exist, but they lack the multigenerational, centralized presence of the Irish Travellers.

Some Travellers have, over the years, been convicted of crimes, but that needn't suggest they're all criminals. Members of any group can engage in criminal enterprise. The Travellers are, however, a uniquely tight-knit clan with long-lived traditions and are a culturally unique part of the South Carolina Midlands—with members who have committed some distinctly different crimes.

Over the decades since their arrival in the United States, the families have tended to live and travel together. Mike Carroll, a Traveller who wrote of their history, said the ethnic group numbers fewer than 5,000. They share a list of surnames; marriages are often arranged within the community. Marriages and funerals are commemorated as a community, and ceremonies traditionally have been held at annual gatherings at a Nashville Catholic church that sits conveniently between the three largest settlements. Originally known as Irish Nomads, the families now congregate in three homeplaces: in White Settlement, Texas (west of Fort Worth); in Memphis, Tennessee; and in North Augusta—reportedly the largest community, with about 1,400 residents.

They tend to stay separate from non-Travellers. But that separateness can lead to suspicion and misunderstanding. And when one of their group is arrested, it tends to make headlines. As journalist J.R. Lind pointed out, "Oftentimes news coverage and press releases from district attorneys and police departments focus on the fact it's Travellers, rather than on the crimes themselves."

In one 1993 case, a young woman claimed she was attacked, raped and robbed by an assailant while she was vacationing at Disney World's Caribbean Beach Resort hotel. She reported the incident to the Orange County Sheriff's Office and also filed a lawsuit against Disney for negligence. As investigators interviewed her and followed up on leads, they noticed holes in her story. Then an informant, apparently angry over her deception and that she was suing Disney to get money, called to tell investigators her story was a hoax. The victim's brother was the mastermind—and had attacked her with a stick. The investigator said, "She was beaten pretty badly. They made it look very realistic."

Because Disney was the target of the fraud, the story made headlines. Accounts linked the fraudsters to their Traveller roots.

Originally, members of the community traveled to work the land and trade horses or as tinkerers, fixing pots and other household and farm items. As the world changed, they opted to settle permanently in enclaves. And they found other, more modern versions of horse-trading. One activity is an updated version of the ancient practice of tontine, where participants pool money and the surviving member wins all. The new version is to buy life insurance policies on family members and collect benefits when they die. That's legal as long as the insured consents to the policy and the purchaser has an "insurable interest," which means the policy holder would suffer a loss if the insured died—loss of income because a business partner dies or loss of companionship or support if a family member dies. Travellers often pool their money to insure grandparents or cousins or other relations.

A problem arose in 2014, though, when Bernard "Little Joe" Gorman and his father of White Settlement, Texas, insured their housekeeper for $1 million and sold her policy to a relative. She was murdered, and Gorman eventually pleaded guilty to conspiracy to commit murder. His father didn't live to stand trial.

Nothing so violent occurred in a recent South Carolina insurance-sharing scheme, but the size of the fraud and the large number of defendants grabbed headlines. According to filings with the U.S. District Court in Columbia, a two-year federal investigation centered on misrepresentations of income and assets on applications to purchase cars or insurance, on food stamp and Medicare fraud and on fraudulent income tax refunds and money laundering.

The U.S. attorney in Columbia worked with the FBI, IRS, U.S. marshals and state and local law enforcement to build the cases. The first charges were brought in January 2016; by August 2017, fifty-two members of the community had entered guilty pleas. Most of the charges were brought under the federal Racketeer Influenced and Corrupt Organizations Act (RICO), first created to crack mafia organizations in New York and other large cities. As reporter John Monk with *The State* pointed out, the surnames on the indictments illustrate the family relationships: "seven Carrolls, seven Sherlocks, three O'Haras, three Rileys, two Gormans and two Macks."

Blaming a group for the criminal activity of a few members can be unfair profiling, but the Travellers' voluntary isolation from mainstream society made identifying their members easy. And the crimes attributed to the Travellers have been headline-grabbing and anything but boring.

The Minister and the Hitman

Televangelists and faith healers aren't unknown in the South. Some are better known than others, and some become famous for reasons other than their remarkable preaching or their strong faith. In April 1979, a spiritual healer based in Greenwood began working his way toward a stint in state prison in Columbia, not as a prison minister but as a resident.

Known for selling his healing T-shirts, his albums of religious music and for his resemblance, some said, to Elvis, the Reverend Leroy Jenkins had moved around a lot but settled in South Carolina for a time. His big moneymaker was his miracle water. According to journalist Dave Ghose, Leroy preached on his television show about a "lady [who] said she took it and poured it in the yard of a house she wanted, and God gave her that house." Miracles aside, regulators in West Virginia said the water was contaminated and could cause gastric distress and diarrhea.

After suspicious fires at properties Jenkins owned in Ohio and South Carolina, a federal undercover Alcohol, Tobacco and Firearms (ATF) agent took a job as Jenkins's bodyguard. The investigation conducted by ATF, SLED and the local police and sheriff caught something they hadn't expected to hear. On profanity-laced audiotapes recorded by the undercover agent, Jenkins shared plans to burn down the houses of a Highway Patrol officer and a local businessman.

On April 17, 1979, Jenkins was taken into custody for conspiring with two men—one, the undercover agent. A news photo captured him in a jail jumpsuit, one hand casually in his pocket, the other waving at the photographer as he walked along a hallway with law officers. Jenkins was also charged with threatening an *Anderson Independent* reporter over a series of articles with the headline "Who Is Leroy Jenkins? Crusade with a $3 Million Income" (over $12 million today).

That a faith healer would solicit arson was odd enough, but the motive? In March, the Highway Patrol officer had arrested Jenkins's nineteen-year-old daughter for speeding, driving without a license and disorderly conduct. She was also convicted of resisting arrest and sentenced to six months in jail, plus fines and probation.

Before the hired fire-setters with their cans of gasoline could damage the patrolman's house, officers intercepted them. At one point in the criminal proceedings, attorney F. Lee Bailey represented Jenkins in his federal suit attempting to set bail. A jury later convicted him—to the surprise and dismay of his eight children and his many supporters. Jenkins served over five years of his twelve-year prison sentence and was released from probation in 1988. He left South Carolina for Ohio and Florida, where he died in 2017.

Fire at the Farm

Public awareness of the 1980s Farm Crisis—significant enough to earn a capital-lettered title—focused on the massive farms in the midwestern United States. But the farming regions in South Carolina were also hard-hit by high interest rates on loans for land and equipment, steep oil prices, changing government farm policy and droughts. Some farmers weathered the storm, but one man didn't have the chance.

On June 10, 1987, tobacco farmer Billy E. Graham was found dead in his bedroom, his rambling two-story white farmhouse in flames. The medical examiner determined that Graham died as a result of the fire, listing the cause of death as thermal burns and carbon monoxide poisoning from smoke inhalation. The fire investigation showed no clear signs of arson, and

Main Street in Olanta, South Carolina. *Courtesy of Evanoco via Wikimedia Commons.*

the death was ruled accidental. Fifty-nine-year-old Graham was laid to rest, and weeds began to take over the once well-kept lawn around the burned-out shell of his house.

The rumors didn't rest, though. Olanta was a small town, only seven hundred people in the 1980s, located closer to Sumter than to Florence in an area known at the time for expansive tobacco farms. Prosperous farmers would lease land to expand their own operations from families who'd given up farming. Graham was among the prosperous ones, farming around three thousand acres and especially noted for his prize horses. But when hard times hit, he couldn't repay loans to the Federal Land Bank and the Farmers Home Administration (FmHA) or get financing to buy his year's tobacco allotments from other farmers. Then a business deal with two friends went bad—and that failure looked orchestrated, an attempt to take over his holdings.

Graham successfully sued his friends—Citizen's Bank of Olanta president Charlie Dorn Smith and Roger D. "Bill" Prince, his foster son and business partner. One of several lawsuits alleged that Smith and Prince hatched a plan to take over Graham's farm by forcing a default on a large loan from Smith's bank. Graham had also filed a federal lawsuit, but he died shortly before that trial was scheduled to start.

Despite what was whispered about Graham's death and the allegedly crooked dealings of his friends, the investigation was closed—until Charles McCray started talking to investigators.

At first, the February 1988 arrest of McCray, a local handyman, had nothing to do with Graham's death. On January 30, 1988, two hunters in Clarendon County found a shallow grave and the decomposing body of twenty-six-year-old Paul "Junior" Bradley. Word got to investigators that Bradley's friend McCray had been drinking and bragging to another friend that he'd killed him. After McCray's arrest, he started talking about how he'd been hired to kill Graham.

Maybe his involvement had weighed on his conscience, but he soon admitted he shot Graham, stole pistols from his house and set it on fire.

Graham's body was exhumed. A second autopsy showed that he had been shot twice with a .22-caliber weapon. The small entrance wound behind his ear was hard to spot, given the damage from the fire. The slugs were lodged in his brain, so no exit wound existed—which would have been larger and easier to see.

Sheriff Barnes said he'd alerted the first pathologist about his suspicions that the death might be murder, but the pathologist failed to X-ray the body—a routine procedure that would have located the two bullets in Graham's brain. The sheriff was blunt in his assessment: "The pathologist screwed up."

Finger-pointing could be expected. But so could attempts to cover up or keep things quiet. In a small town, people have to continue to live and work together. They know that memories are long, and the mistake forgiven today might earn some grace when the next mistake is on the other side.

In May 1991, the criminal trial of three men charged in Graham's death began: the former bank president, the foster son and the handyman, Charles McCray. Settling on what charges each would face was not easy—for the prosecutor or for the jury. McCray was charged with capital murder and eligible for the death penalty; he was already serving a life sentence for the murder of his friend Junior Bradley, the death that had originally drawn authorities' attention to him. Murder charges against Smith and Prince were dropped, but they had given McCray money to kill Graham, so they faced charges of conspiracy to commit murder, accessory before the fact of murder and solicitation to commit murder.

Though the prosecution isn't required to supply a motive in a murder case, money was clearly at the root of this killing. Smith, Prince and another defendant in the land swindle lawsuit had been ordered to pay Graham around $400,000. They had yet to pay him and were appealing the verdict. In addition, Prince had a $500,000 life insurance policy on Graham, the man who'd taken him in as a foster son and raised him.

Feelings ran high in the close-knit community, and security was tight at the courthouse. Judge Ralph King Anderson—one of the state's preeminent circuit court judges, a former member of the state House of Representatives and elected in 1996 to serve on the state's court of appeals—served as trial judge. Picking a jury had its challenges; the judge disqualified one juror who'd written on his juror information form, "I am prejudice, bigot and sexist."

The jury convicted all three men. McCray was sentenced to an additional life term but avoided Death Row. Prince and Smith were also convicted, with charges of at least ten years each.

Two of the men convicted were prominent businessmen and longtime friends of the man they'd arranged to kill. Others had been caught up in the investigation's net, but they weren't prosecuted. At the end of it all, questions still remained. What went wrong? And why? Was it nothing more than greed? Was the deal-making too complicated? The money too good? Had a mistake not forgiven in the past led to retaliation? The real answers likely never made it into a court report or a newspaper article, but the speculation continued to circle long after the judge's gavel cracked down for the last time.

8

POLITICAL SCANDALS

The 1980s became the decade of political scandal for South Carolina politicians at state and national levels. Grainy undercover footage of men sitting around in hotel rooms talking about legalizing dog- and horse-track betting or selling drugs or helping someone with immigration issues while stuffing wads of cash in their pockets became routine nightly news fare, so common that some viewers and voters became inured to the images.

But long after the arrests and prosecutions, the battles still raged over the extent of the corruption, its effect on government, the best solutions to clean up the mess and whether the prosecutors had been overly zealous or just doing a difficult job.

The answers and solutions still aren't clear. While the players in the scandals represented districts from around the state, Columbia, as the seat of state politics, was ground zero for most of the investigation, the court cases and the aftermath.

LOST TRUST

In 1989, the statehouse scandal known as Operation Lost Trust—the FBI's code name for the investigation—became public. The legal wranglings would continue for another decade. The federal investigation was launched in 1988 to look at reports of illegal drug use among South Carolina legislators. It soon

South Carolina State House in 1960, part of the Historic American Buildings Survey.
Courtesy of Jack E. Boucher and Library of Congress Prints and Photographs Division.

turned into an exposé of bribery, corruption and vote-buying. Eventually, eleven lobbyists and seventeen legislators—from both sides of the political aisle—were caught in the net. All but one was convicted or pleaded guilty before trial to offenses including bribery, extortion and drug offenses. In the book *Presumed Guilty*, Tim Wilkes of Winnsboro, the sole target of the investigation acquitted of his charges, told about the overwhelming tidal wave of power the federal government can bring to bear on a single target.

The federal court of appeals overturned five of the convictions based on problems with the jury instructions given by the trial judge. Three of those were eventually convicted in new trials. The federal prosecution team, headed by U.S. Attorney Bart Daniel, also came in for criticism for overzealousness, for "allowing political pressure to derail his investigation" and for allegedly withholding information from the court. Watching the fur fly, particularly over the years it took for the investigations and trials to come to a close, left most in the state with little understanding of who or what to believe.

When the investigation opened, the first target was the influential lobbyist Ron Cobb; he was caught buying a kilo of cocaine in an undercover sting operation. Cobb agreed to turn informant and to tape conversations with legislators willing to sell their votes in a controversial push to legalize pari-mutuel betting on dog- and horse-racing in the state.

Once arrests were made and details of the investigation began airing on the nightly news, videotapes of the deals showed promises made about votes and hundred-dollar bills and Super Bowl tickets changing hands. Ron Cobb operated from a room overlooking the statehouse as the hidden camera recorded his transactions with colleagues. He smoked cigars, clinked cocktail glasses and famously said, "It's a bidness doing pleasure with you."

As a result of the disclosures and scandal, the state legislature wrote far-reaching new state ethics rules regulating campaign contributions and lobbyists' activities. Under the new rules, lobbyists can't treat an individual legislator to something as inconsequential as a coffee or doughnut. But in retrospect, did anything change? Yes and no, according to political observers. In a *Post and Courier* article twenty years after the dust settled, Bart Daniel, the crusading former U.S attorney, said lobbyists have actually thanked him for cleaning things up, that they sometimes felt like they were being extorted to vote a certain way.

But John Crangle of South Carolina's Common Cause chapter—a national political watchdog group—had a different perspective. He told journalist Andy Brack that not much had changed—instead, he felt it had gotten worse. "The magnitude of the money has increased dramatically." The way the money moves—through political action committees or caucuses—has replaced hundred-dollar bills quietly slipped into pockets. But influence peddling is still part of the currency of political life. In Brack's words, it's not as flamboyant, in-your-face or no-holds-barred as in 1990 but still part of the political landscape. Brack saw many legislators who "seem to head to Columbia with noble goals of making a difference." But rules don't create uniformly good morals for those who are elected.

ABSCAM

Before Operation Lost Trust, an even higher profile political scandal unfolded in the nation's capital. And it featured a congressman who, only a few years earlier, had been a rapidly rising star in Columbia's statehouse. John Jenrette was elected to represent his Myrtle Beach district in 1964. Eight years later, he stepped down from his state post to run for a seat in the U.S. House of Representatives. John was charming and canny. Not the southern good ol' boy of 1970s stereotypes, he championed Black people, women, blue-collar workers and the elderly, and he became the first congressional freshman to serve on the House Majority leadership team. His political future in Washington was even rosier than his time in Columbia's legislature until he became one of seven congressional members caught up in the infamous Abscam probe.

ABSCAM was the FBI's code name for an investigation that started as an investigation into stolen art and ended with, as the FBI's history describes, "everything from mobsters hocking stolen paintings and fake securities in the Big Apple to politicians peddling influence in the nation's capitol."

To lure in the dealers in stolen art, the FBI set up Abdul Enterprises (AB[dul]SCAM), with a wealthy but fake sheik interested in buying art. The operation transitioned from a successful $1 million art recovery to a $600 million securities fraud case to an Atlantic City bribery case involving a

Hidden camera video from the FBI's ABSCAM undercover sting investigation. *Courtesy of the FBI.*

gaming license, then on to Washington for a $100,000 payment in a "private legislation" asylum case. As the sting operation grew in scope, the wild tales of what the sheik wanted and why he had to do it under the table and how much he was willing to pay continued to morph into bigger and more fantastic schemes.

As with many high-profile scandals, the initial fascination with the unfolding criminal tomfoolery later turned to a questioning assessment of the tactics used to capture the crooks. In 1981, a Department of Justice workshop on Abscam Entrapment was offered, focusing on three aspects of the Abscam "sting" that had been criticized: how charges were leaked before the grand jury took action, how members of Congress who would be tempted by bribes were selected and whether the offers of bribes were entrapment. Abscam introduced the legal concept of "entrapment" to the common vocabulary.

Generally, entrapment can be used as a defense in a criminal prosecution if (1) the government induced the crime and (2) the defendant lacked the predisposition to commit the crime on his own. Inducement goes beyond just suggesting the idea; it includes persuasion or even coercion to do something the defendant wouldn't have been inclined to do. Even after dissection in U.S. Supreme Court cases, the lines are difficult to discern. Was it permissible to target members of Congress based on tips that they would consider selling political favors? Or was the offer just too good to refuse, making it easy for the government agents to entrap otherwise innocent or susceptible targets?

In the end, the convictions of one senator; six House members; the mayor of Camden, New Jersey; some Philadelphia city politicians; and assorted criminals were upheld by the courts. John Jenrette was the only true southerner caught in the sweep (excluding one fellow from Florida).

In 2017, the case was loosely portrayed in the movie *American Hustle*. In the list of political scandals that the *Daily Beast* noted in its review of the movie, Abscam wasn't the first—or even the flashiest or most damaging—in our scandal history, when measured against the robber barons and their Gilded Age excesses, the Teapot Dome scandal, Huey Long's reign in Louisiana or Richard Nixon and the Watergate break-in. But it held its own fascination.

A contrite John Jenrette appeared at his sentencing in 1983, three years after his conviction. At the hearing, even federal attorney Reid Weingarten had kind words to say about Jenrette as a "man of obvious talent" who was "genuinely sorry for what he has done." But Weingarten didn't downplay the damage Jenrette had done to citizens' faith in the political system.

At sentencing, Judge John Garrett Penn expressed sympathy and said he saw "no evidence that you went out and looked for a way to sell your office." The judge wished Jenrette had taken a different path when presented with the temptation of a $50,000 bribe—but he hadn't. He sentenced Jenrette to two years in prison, five years' probation and fines of $20,000.

After his release from prison, Jenrette worked in sales and promoted various business schemes in the United States and Europe. His later years in South Carolina were quiet, but as players in political scandals go, Jenrette was never boring or mundane—in part because of his ex-wife Rita Jenrette, whom he married eighteen months after he moved to Washington.

After his conviction in 1980, his beautiful blond wife divorced him and began making her own way in the world. She was featured in *Playboy*'s April 1981 issue and wrote a sizzling memoir, *My Capitol Secrets*; tried an acting career in Hollywood, with roles on *The Equalizer*, *Fantasy Island* and *Zombie Island Massacre*; published *Conglomerate*, a romantic thriller, in 1986; worked in New York as a television correspondent for *A Current Affair* in the late 1980s; and sold real estate. In that role, she met her prince—literally.

Rita's rather chaste photos for *Playboy* created one of the most iconic moments of the Abscam aftermath, made more interesting by her

Steps to the U.S. Capitol in Washington. Did the columns shelter a tryst—or not? *Courtesy of Louis Velazquez on Unsplash.*

accompanying article. During a late-night congressional session, she and John snuck out behind a pillar on the Capitol steps. "He took my hand and led me into the shadows, and we made love on the marble steps that overlook the monuments and the city below." She said, "He was the most romantic man I had ever known." That got tongues talking.

Perhaps even more shocking was when, thirty years later, she claimed that's really not what happened. She got carried away in her interview, she said. With tongue in cheek, the *Washington Post*'s Reliable Source gossip column put her retraction in context with other Washington political scandals: "Well, *this* changes everything! Imagine if Monica Lewinsky's blue Gap dress actually came from Saks. Or if Fanne Foxe jumped into McMillan Reservoir instead of the Tidal Basin. Or if the Watergate break-in happened somewhere else, and we could no longer call every scandal Something-gate."

The statement that tried to tone down her colorful history came when Rita Jenrette was interviewed about the latest phase of her storied life. While working in New York real estate in 2003, she met, fell in love with and married Prince Nicolò Boncompagni Ludovisi of Italy. Until his death in 2018, they worked together to preserve his family's historic nine-thousand-square-foot Villa Aurora in Rome. Built in 1570, the massive home is filled with rare artwork, most notably the only known ceiling mural by Caravaggio, uncovered from beneath a layer of paint in 1969. According to *Artnet*, Rita took on the role of preserving her husband's family history, digitizing 150,000 documents from their archives; some were sent to the Vatican for preservation. She knows which cedar tree in the garden Henry James sat under while writing at the villa and has the treasure trove of letters written by Marie Antoinette.

A sixteenth-century structure requires massive and expensive upkeep. Rita began serving as tour guide at the villa to raise money. According to a Rutgers University historian, "The villa was considered hopeless. Rita and her husband stepped in and deserve a lot of credit."

But after the prince's death, his sons by his first marriage were not as complimentary or supportive. His will provided the Villa Aurora for Rita's residence until her death, and she would split the proceeds with her stepsons if the property were sold. The stepsons have contested the will and sought to have the property, which has been in their family since 1621, sold. The estimates of its value—driven in part by the collection of valuable art it holds—ranged from $157 million to $546 million, but as of January 2023, it had failed to sell at auction.

Villa Aurora in Rome, home of Princess Rita Jenrette Ludovisi and her Italian prince. *Courtesy of Lalupa via Wikimedia Commons.*

The seventy-three-year-old princess, who looks much younger than her age, is still a willowy platinum blond with a charming smile, an open frankness and the steely determination that has seen her through a lifetime of adventures. In a 2011 interview with Ariel Levy for the *New Yorker*, the prince described his wife: "She's beautiful, of course, but she's as beautiful inside. She's candid like a child but shrewd like a fox!"

Those caught up in political scandals—even the fairy-tale princesses— seldom have fairy-tale endings.

9

THE LEGISLATIVE DAUGHTERS

DID HE? OR DIDN'T HE?

Forensic technology continues to make amazing leaps. Not only can cell-tower pings pinpoint the location of a single phone but they also can identify every phone active within a "geo-fenced" area, for instance, around a crime scene. DNA technology has moved from requiring large biologic samples and months for testing and the need to have a suspect to match the sample against. Now, a DNA profile may be obtained if someone merely touches a person or object, and a suspect can be located by a "reverse build" of a genetic family tree connecting an unnamed perpetrator's DNA to that of a family member. So it's unsettling to read cases where none of those techniques were available and the solution wasn't found—or worse yet, the wrong solution was reached.

What if the wrong man confessed to a crime but police had no way to test that confession? Surely a confession alone must be enough to establish guilt. But crime annals are rife with cases where a false confession came from someone too young or mentally limited or easily swayed or tricked. Rational people ask why someone would confess to a crime he didn't commit. But if an interrogator says, "You know you did it. If you just tell us the truth, you can go home," that could sound enticing to someone not sophisticated enough to recognize the ruse or too exhausted from hours of questioning, perhaps without food or water or a cigarette break.

Or perhaps the confession came after a beating. The rubber hose in an interrogation room away from prying eyes is not just a figment of a screenwriter's imagination. Beatings and torture to elicit confessions were reality, though public sentiment and more enlightened law enforcement practices began banning their use. The watershed year was 1937. Thanks to the U.S. Supreme Court case *Brown v. Mississippi*, involuntary confessions violate due process of law.

Changes in the law didn't mean the tactic disappeared. Taped interviews with former Los Angeles police detective Mark Fuhrman surfaced in 1995, during the O.J. Simpson trial, in which he claimed to have beaten suspects. He called it the "77th lie detector test," referring to the 77th Street police station. Those tape recordings were made by a screenwriter, so Fuhrman could have been embellishing his stories, but few doubted they held a kernel of truth.

Most cringe at the thought of violence toward a witness or suspect, but what if a child had been murdered in a truly horrible way? What if a likely suspect quickly became obvious? What if he had already served time for murders in Georgia and been released early, ignoring a statement by state prison psychologists that he might be a danger to himself and others? Could an extreme case prompt extreme, though indefensible solutions?

On December 18, 1970, school in Sumter let out early for the Christmas holidays. Temperatures in the sixties felt more springlike than a harbinger of Christmas. Thirteen-year-old Margaret "Peg" Cuttino asked her mom if she could walk the few blocks to the elementary school to have lunch with her younger sister. In 1970s Sumter, walking along the street in their quiet neighborhood was commonplace. Why should a parent worry?

Peg was seen walking past the YMCA, almost to the elementary school. Then no one knew where she went. Or how she got there. Or why she disappeared.

Peg seemed a proper and polite young teen, not one who'd take off or party or lie to her mother about lunch with her little sister. But by midafternoon, she wasn't home.

Sumter was a small town. And people knew the Cuttino family—her father represented the district in the state legislature. Perhaps the reaction would've been the same for any missing girl, but the response was small-town quick: announcements on the radio, search efforts launched, community prayers for her safe return, a horseback patrol of the woods near town. The sheriff sent out a nationwide alert, fearing she may have been kidnapped. Still, they had no word from or sight of five-foot-two, dark-haired Peg wearing her modest white skirt, blue blouse and polka-dotted sash.

The days wore on, and the community's concern grew increasingly fearful. On December 30, two air force officers bicycling along trails in Manchester State Forest spotted what could have been a discarded mannequin covered in leaves and tree limbs—except it wore the polka-dot sash featured in the numerous news broadcasts of the search for Peg Cuttino.

Medical examiners from Charleston's Medical University of South Carolina came to the scene, along with investigators. Their examination showed Peg had probably died on the day she disappeared—twelve days earlier. She'd been bludgeoned, probably with a tire iron or similar object, and she'd been sexually assaulted. The experts' examination yielded a controversial piece of evidence: the sperm in the body had not degraded, as they would expect given the warm weather and the time elapsed. Still, they stuck with their assessment of the date of death.

The investigation was extensive and included SLED agents along with the sheriff's office and Sumter police. They followed a reported 1,500 leads, but no clear suspects emerged—until Sheriff J.B. "Red" Carter from over in Baxley, Georgia, called J.P. Strom, head of SLED, South Carolina's statewide law enforcement agency. Operating much like the FBI does on the federal level, SLED investigates at the invitation of local law enforcement. Sheriff Carter notified SLED that he had an inmate in his jail making some interesting comments about a case in Sumter.

That's where the case either begins to look solved or turns into a hash of a mess, depending on the point of view.

Junior Pierce, as he was known, endured a poor and abused childhood. Perhaps a later head injury precipitated his criminal acts—mostly petty crimes, until he killed eighteen-year-old Ann Goodwin while burglarizing a North Augusta home in June 1970.

According to the official account of his crimes, he next encountered Peg Cuttino near the YMCA in Sumter, and his spree continued from there, back into Georgia, with store robberies, a rape, at least six murders and the severe beating of a five-year-old witness. He was captured in May 1971, following yet another store robbery. Police found evidence in his possession to support his confessions.

But he was also one of a special breed known to law enforcement: the serial confessor. Pierce—who had made an art of dramatic, over-the-top confessions for purposes that few could discern—said he'd driven to Sumter to "rob and steal" and stopped for something to eat in downtown Sumter. Outside the restaurant, he rescued Peg from an altercation with a young man. She offered to ride with Pierce—which caused those who heard the story and knew Peg to raise an eyebrow. Why would a girl like Peg ride off with a scruffy, rough-edged guy like Pierce?

He said he drove her to the county landfill. When she started crying and wanted to go home, he got scared, took a tire iron from the trunk of his car and hit her repeatedly. Then he drove about half a mile away and buried her in a shallow grave in some woods.

So much about his story sounded fantastical: that a boy outside a downtown restaurant grabbed a length of chain from his car and threatened Pierce when Pierce intervened to help Peg; that Pierce pulled a gun and threatened the boy, who backed down; that Peg got into his car and rode off with him. Why had no one in small, close-knit—even nosy—Sumter not called the police? No one reported seeing the incident in busy downtown Sumter on the last day of school, during the Christmas shopping rush and in pleasant weather, which drew people outside.

Why not dump her at the landfill, where he said they were parked? Why bother taking her elsewhere?

Pierce's IQ became a central issue in prosecuting him. He tested at barely 70, significantly below the average IQ score of 100 and in a range often demonstrating someone with childlike understanding of consequences and easily manipulated.

Junior Pierce's elaborate and outlandish confession helped solve a difficult case for people in Sumter. But not everyone was convinced of his guilt.

Courts have ruled that investigators can use ruses when interrogating suspects. They can claim that evidence—such as a fingerprint, DNA or an eyewitness—puts the suspect at the scene. They can claim someone else has implicated him. In theory, an innocent person won't cave under the pressure of fake evidence and falsely confess. The basic guidelines for using ruses were set in a 1969 U.S. Supreme Court case: "Strategic deception of the suspect by police, where it is not sufficient to overbear the suspect's will but merely prompts him to act from a consciousness of guilt, does not make a statement involuntary."

Stephanie Simon in the *Los Angeles Times* summarized where the often-wavy lines are drawn for interrogators:

> *For guidance, officers must turn to case law—which provides a confusing, and sometimes contradictory, jumble of rules:*

> *Detectives cannot promise you leniency in exchange for a confession. But they can mention that courts look favorably on cooperative defendants.*

They cannot threaten you or your family. But they can say you will make it easier on your loved ones by talking.

And they are not supposed to play off religious beliefs by suggesting that lying will doom you to hell. But they can tell you a guilty conscience will haunt your dreams.

But not everyone has the same mental capacity to detect tricks and ruses. Some want to please their interrogators. Was Pierce, with his IQ score ranked in the range of "mental retardation" under the standards of the time, easily overcome by those tactics? Or, though intellectually limited, was he a skilled manipulator? Some who heard the tales he told, making himself sound more important than he really was, believed that he thought it was a game to confess.

Before Sheriff Carter in Georgia made the phone call that first connected Pierce with Peg's disappearance, Carrie LeNoir spoke with investigators. Her husband ran a small family store in the Horatio farming community northwest of Sumter, not far from Shaw Air Force Base. Carrie helped in the store and was the part-time postmistress, as well as a volunteer firefighter who often drove the truck to local fires. And she proved to be an indefatigable advocate for what she believed was right. Carrie reported seeing an unfamiliar car with two boys and a young girl in it at the country store. They didn't see many strangers in Horatio, but Carrie hadn't yet heard the news about Peg.

Welcome sign to Horatio, South Carolina, home of the LeNoir Store. *Courtesy of Efy96001 via Wikimedia Commons.*

The historic LeNoir Store on Horatio-Hagood Road, on the National Register of Historic Places. *Courtesy of Efy96001 via Wikimedia Commons.*

The Sumter County Courthouse. *Courtesy of Blackoffee via Wikimedia Commons.*

The car returned that afternoon, without the girl and with the boys acting excited or agitated. When Peg's photo appeared in the local newspaper, Carrie LeNoir's husband said, "That girl was in the store." He'd gotten a good look at her, and this was on the day after Peg's disappearance, the day after the medical examiners later said Peg had to be dead. Carrie hadn't gotten a clear look at the girl near the unfamiliar car, but her hair was shorter than she remembered Peg Cuttino's hair. The next day, she learned Peg had recently cut her hair to shoulder-length. That and the rest of the scene—the unknown boys, with the girl and then alone and the unfamiliar car—was enough to convince Carrie that what she'd seen was critically important.

She called, and two detectives came to talk with her. She remembered them listening, closing their notebooks and thanking her for her time. If Pierce, despite his confession, seemed an unlikely and illogical suspect, Carrie LeNoir's account clearly offered another possible scenario to explain Peg's murder. But she wasn't sure how much credence the detectives gave her story—and she didn't know about the hundreds of other witnesses who'd come forward with something to report.

Investigators felt they had the evidence they needed. In a March 1973 trial that lasted less than two days, William "Junior" Pierce was convicted of the murder. He was already a proven murderer and rapist. Despite the shakiness of the case against him and the elements that defied logic, he'd done plenty of bad things. Peg's parents, the town of Sumter and the officials searching for her killer needed a way to end their nightmare. And Pierce already had a life sentence in Georgia.

Carrie LeNoir and others crusaded to have Pierce exonerated for Peg's murder, and Carrie wrote a book in 1992 detailing the contradictions and questions about the evidence. Despite the doubts, the state supreme court upheld Pierce's conviction in 1974, and no one else was ever charged.

For his other crimes, Junior Pierce spent almost fifty years in a Georgia prison, where he died in May 2010, without ever transferring to a South Carolina prison.

Even with his string of crimes ranging from store robberies to rape and murder and his lifetime spent in prison, Pierce was not a familiar name in true crime circles—until a character with his name appeared on the second season of Netflix's *Mindhunter*, which fictionalized the origins of the FBI's Behavioral Analysis Unit and its profilers. A *Toronto Sun* article described him: "Junior Pierce was one of those killers the U.S. south breeds like the kudzu that grows like wildfire alongside Dixie's highways."

A Family Divided

Just before ten o'clock on the night of June 12, 1994, a sheriff's deputy and a state Highway Patrol trooper responded to a call about a car in a ditch on the road to Little Mountain. As they drove up to the scene outside Prosperity, the damage they could see to the small gray sedan was slight, so they weren't expecting to find a body inside. But this wasn't one of South Carolina's roughly one thousand annual auto fatalities. The young woman inside had been beaten—with a fist, they first thought, though it turned out to be a handgun—and struck brutally on the neck with a heavy object.

Newberry is a small town—about fifteen thousand residents—and folks tend to at least recognize one another, even if they aren't close friends. It didn't take long to learn that the thirty-six-year-old victim, Vickie Lander Beckham, was the daughter of James Lander, the area's state senator, and the daughter-in-law of former Episcopal bishop William Beckham. The investigation would be important because of the families involved and sensitive because one of the first suspects was Vickie's husband, Stephen.

Most homicide investigations naturally start with those closest to the victim. Statistics support that as a logical first step. The Beckhams were living separately—she stayed with her parents, he lived in a house trailer behind his parents' home—and they shared custody of their three children. The couple had been having problems for a while, mostly centered on Stephen's extracurricular activities during his many golf outings to Myrtle Beach. Vickie had apparently first learned about his drug use and late nights at strip clubs about five years earlier. The high school sweethearts first separated at that time but made attempts to save their marriage. He seemed to care about his kids but didn't seem willing to give up his party life.

To residents of Newberry, the investigation dragged on. Stephen hadn't been arrested, so who could have done this? Was a serial killer setting up shop in the area? Had a random killer passed through, someone authorities would never identify? Witnesses had seen a man and a gold-colored Chevrolet on Little Mountain Road near the accident scene. Police had a composite sketch of the man, and no one thought it looked like Stephen Beckham. The questions lingered for a year before an arrest was made.

Some likely felt relieved that they didn't recognize the suspect's name; Richard Anderson wasn't from Newberry. Some outsider had killed Vickie. But when Stephen Beckham was also arrested and charged with kidnapping and murder, the mood in Newberry changed. Now the case was close to home. But how was this possible?

The Newberry County Courthouse. *Courtesy of Chanilim714 via Wikimedia Commons.*

The gold Chevy had been identified as one often parked in front of Smugglers, a topless bar or gentlemen's club in Myrtle Beach. The car belonged to the club's owner. In June 1994, he'd loaned it to his employee, a bouncer named Richard Anderson.

On July 11, 1995, soon after his arrest, Richard Anderson moved the proceedings along quickly. He pleaded guilty and agreed to testify against Stephen Beckham in exchange for avoiding the risk of the death penalty.

A year later, as they prepared for trial, solicitor (as prosecutors or district attorneys are known in South Carolina) Townes Jones added to his team the experienced Knox McMahon from a solicitor's office in another circuit. Knox had worked with Donnie Myers, one of the nation's "deadliest prosecutors," who'd won thirty-nine death sentences (some in retrials for cases overturned by the appellate court, four of those overturned for "overzealous" closing argument by Myers).

For his defense, Stephen's family hired two of South Carolina's most notable criminal trial attorneys: Dick Harpootlian, a former circuit solicitor and future state senator, and Jack Swerling, a veteran of more than 150 criminal defenses and dubbed "Mr. Murder" by the *National Law Journal*. The two had attended Clemson at the same time and recently formed a law partnership.

Stephen's trial started on September 20, 1996. The jury was brought from Oconee County—the publicity and the deep connections of both families raised reasonable questions about impartiality in Newberry. Because the jurors were away from home and sequestered, the court convened even on Sunday.

At trial, the sordid details became public for the first time. Stephen didn't give pretrial interviews or tell his version in court, but others told what they knew while his stellar defense team parried as best they could. He had financial problems—in particular, state and federal tax liens totaling over $65,000 (about $125,000 today). The defense pointed out that, because the debt was shared with Vickie, her death made him liable for the full amount—hardly a motive, they said. But she had a $100,000 life insurance policy payable to him (about $200,000 today). He had scratches on his back, and a visitor at his parents' house saw him walking from the pond about seven o'clock that night.

On the third day, Richard Anderson took the stand and outlined the murder plot they'd concocted at the Myrtle Beach nightclub.

On the afternoon of June 12, he met Stephen at a store off Interstate 26 near Newberry. They left Anderson's car on the rural road where they planned to stage Vickie's car accident, then Anderson rode with Stephen to his trailer and waited in the woods. Anderson testified that Stephen was supposed to deliver to him a dead body and he was supposed to stage the accident by taking the car back to Little Mountain Road, breaking the car window and breaking her neck. Trouble was, Vickie wasn't dead.

Anderson described to the jury the shock of finding her in the car with Stephen, still breathing. After Stephen walked into the woods toward his trailer and left him with his part of the bargain, Anderson struck the blow with a heavy bolt-cutter that crushed her larynx and broke her neck. He then drove to Little Mountain Road, moved her body into position in the driver's seat and set the car rolling toward a steep embankment. But the car veered toward the other side of the road just as Anderson saw the headlights of an approaching car. He knew he had to make his escape.

Stephen hadn't left the promised $5,000 payment in the car for Anderson. According to the *Greenville News* reporter's account, Anderson testified, "I wondered how I let myself get involved in this.…I took for granted that I'd been hung out to dry. I felt like the only thing I could do was to try to make it out of there.…I decided the only thing I could do was get to my car and get the hell out of there."

The details of Vickie's death were difficult for her family to hear. Testimony also showed that this wasn't the first attempt to kill her. Her aunt testified that four days earlier, she'd ridden with Vickie when she delivered the children to Stephen's trailer. She'd overheard Stephen ask Vickie to drop her aunt off and come back alone so they could talk. It was important, he said. Vickie refused. Anderson testified that was the night they'd initially planned her murder, but Stephen couldn't get her alone. Their next opportunity came four days later.

After the three-week trial, the jury retired to deliberate. Seven hours later, they had a verdict: guilty on all counts. During the penalty phase, family members testified for Stephen—and his children were his most compelling witnesses. But the courtroom also heard testimony from a man who'd been jailed with Stephen Beckham as he awaited trial. He said Stephen regretted that he hadn't killed Richard Anderson, that rather than hiring another lawyer, he wanted to take that money and "put it on Richard Anderson's head."

In the sentencing phase, Stephen made his own appeal to the jury. Reporters for *The State* newspaper described the testimony: "'Life in prison doesn't appeal to me,' he said in a hushed and halting statement a few feet from the jury box. 'Dying might be easier for me, but not for my children. I just don't want to hurt my children anymore.' He spoke with his shoulders slightly hunched and nervously rubbed his thumbs against his forefingers." He admitted his involvement with drugs and his "huge mistakes."

Stephen Beckham was sentenced to life with the possibility of parole after thirty years. Anderson was sentenced to life with parole possible after twenty years; he was denied parole at his first hearing because of the violence of the offense and remains incarcerated at this writing.

Two families who loved their children and a small town divided in its loyalties. A father and church official who defended his son on the witness stand so fiercely that the judge had to reprimand him, even promising a contempt charge if it continued. Children testifying that they loved both their mother and their father. Some of the best litigators known to South Carolina courtrooms battling to convince a jury what justice should look like. A father and defendant—the preacher's kid gone wild—standing before his family and friends, his victim's family, news media and the judge and jury who would decide his sentence. Domestic crimes are too common—but some deeply affect not just the families involved but the community that knows and cares about them.

10

SIDE TRIPS, CRIME BITS AND ODDITIES

VICIOUS POLITICS

Lest one think vicious politics are a recent concern, one should revisit Main Street in Columbia on January 15, 1903. N.G. Gonzales, the founder of *The State* newspaper and a well-known and controversial journalist, stepped out of his newspaper offices at 1220 Main Street to walk toward Gervais Street on his way home for a late lunch. As chance had it, he came face to face with Lieutenant Governor James Tillman, in the company of two state senators. Neither the politician nor the journalist would have been happy about the encounter.

Gonzales stepped aside to let the three men pass. At close range, Tillman pulled a Luger pistol from his overcoat pocket and fired, one quick shot that entered and exited Gonzales's gut. A witness heard Tillman say, "You will let me alone now."

Gonzales, still standing and defiant, said, "Shoot again, you coward."

Tillman walked away, but police quickly apprehended him and took him to jail. Gonzales lingered in the hospital but, without modern antibiotics, developed gangrene and died a painful death four days later.

Tillman was the nephew of "Pitchfork" Ben Tillman, a firebrand more popular in rural parts of the state than in Columbia. Gonzales's mother descended from landed aristocracy on Edisto Island; his father fought for Cuban independence. Gonzales and his paper supported the landowners but also advocated for educating Black children and eliminating child labor, while the Tillmans of Edgefield were populists, fighting for the farmers and for continuing racist policies. Their world views couldn't have been more opposed.

Gonzales and his newspaper had long criticized the Tillman faction. During James Tillman's bid for the governorship, the newspaper had called him a debauchee, a criminal and a liar. James lost the election and would vacate the lieutenant governor's office in a few days, when the newly elected governor was sworn in.

Gonzales's funeral was rivaled only by that of former governor General Wade Hampton, who died the year before.

After Gonzales's death, the heated partisanship continued when the indictment of Tillman was slow in coming and when the trial was moved from Columbia to Lexington, seen as a friendlier venue for Tillman.

In a *State* newspaper article on the centenary of the shooting, Donnie Myers, longtime Lexington County prosecutor and student of the case, said, "This was the crime of the century in South Carolina, and it would lead to the trial of the century."

COL. JAMES H. TILLMAN

Photo of Lieutenant Governor James Tillman. *From* Historical Roster and Itinerary of South Carolina Volunteer Troops Who Served in the Late War Between the United States and Spain, *1898, courtesy of Richland Library, Columbia, South Carolina.*

In Tillman's criminal trial, attorneys who faced off against each other included a future governor and the father of a future governor.

To bolster their argument that Tillman could reasonably believe Gonzales was armed and meant him harm, the defense lawyers read to the jury the scathing editorials Gonzales had written about Tillman. Defense lawyers have an old saying that the best defense is that the victim deserved killing and that the defendant was the logical one to do the job. A century later, Myers said Tillman's attorneys turned to the time-honored defense: "What was really argued was that anybody who would write such terrible things about a man needed to be killed, and Tillman was the right man to kill him."

The jury deliberated for twenty hours before the two holdouts for conviction gave in. Tillman was acquitted.

When James Tillman died in 1911, at the age of forty-two, the *State* apparently didn't publish a death notice. Uncle Ben Tillman later said of his nephew that he "had as many brains as any Tillman I ever knew but could not control his passions," which is a noteworthy observation coming from a man known as a "firebrand."

Monument honoring slain newspaper editor N.G. Gonzales. *Courtesy of R. Maxey Collection, Richland Library, Columbia, South Carolina.*

James Tillman lived to see a stately monument honoring his nemesis and victim placed at the corner of Senate and Sumter Streets, across from the statehouse. The inscription named him a "martyr to free speech in South Carolina."

PROFESSOR GREENER

Statue honoring Richard T. Greener—lawyer, professor and librarian—outside the Thomas Cooper Library on the University of South Carolina campus. *Photo by Cathy Pickens.*

In 2009, in a house scheduled for demolition in the Englewood neighborhood in Chicago, Rufus McDonald rescued a steamer trunk full of old books and papers from a dumpster. He didn't know what kind of treasure he'd saved.

The papers once belonged to Richard T. Greener, an African American with an impressive list of firsts, among them the first Black man to graduate from Harvard and the first to serve on the faculty and as librarian at the University of South Carolina, where he organized books and papers left in disarray after the Civil War. He also earned a law degree from USC and was admitted to the South Carolina Bar in 1877, while also teaching college courses ranging from philosophy to Latin and Greek to international and constitutional law.

He fled Columbia in the face of a threatened assassination attempt. He went on to serve in diplomatic roles in Bombay and Vladivostok and as dean of the law school at Howard University.

Greener's wife changed the family's last name to Greene when he became estranged from them—in part because of his continuing activism after the Civil War. One of his daughters, Belle de Costa Greene, worked as personal librarian for J.P Morgan; she was responsible for his rare book collection and served as first director of the Morgan Library.

In 2013, USC acquired for its archives two of the documents rescued from the trunk found in Chicago: Greener's 1876 law degree and his license to practice law in South Carolina.

COP KILLER, ESCAPEE AND TV FUGITIVE

On the Wednesday before Thanksgiving in 1985, Sam Wodke left Columbia to conduct some business in Greenville. Late-night shoppers at the Family Mart on Greenville's East North Street were stopping by for final ingredients for the next day's feast. They hadn't expected, at that near-midnight hour, to be faced with two determined armed robbers. The *Greenville News* reported that one of the store employees quit the next week after a "cocky, confident and unafraid Rusty Corvette put a gun barrel between his eyes." Corvette and mastermind Sam Wodke made away with about $8,000. They escaped with Wodke's son Richard sitting in the back of the getaway Chevette; Richard had stayed in the car and refused to join them when he realized what his dad and Corvette had planned.

Store employees called in a description of the car and the license plate number. Dennis Eubanks, a Greenville County Sheriff's deputy, saw the car only moments later. He and Constable Valdon O. Keith, an unpaid volunteer with the sheriff's office, positioned their cruiser as a roadblock. Wodke pulled up beside the cruiser and fired a borrowed 9mm semiautomatic weapon out the window. Constable Keith was killed.

Wodke drove from Greenville to his Lexington County home, where he ditched the borrowed car. The next day, on Thanksgiving, authorities expected to find him near an address on South Waccamaw Street in Columbia, but he didn't appear. The next evening, some officers recognized him enjoying dinner with a woman at the Hungry Fisherman on the Congaree River in West Columbia. The couple were surprised when they walked out and were met by officers who had surrounded the restaurant.

After his arrest, Wodke, with his shoulder-length curling hair, his self-assured swagger and his Mephistophelian mustache and goatee, told any reporter who'd listen that he was innocent. He and Corvette worked out a plan to blame nineteen-year-old Richard Wodke for the shooting. With their records, the punishment would be more severe for them than for a teenager with no record—the young man who'd played it smart and stayed in the backseat of the getaway car.

Corvette took a plea deal and testified. Richard hadn't wanted to testify against his own father, but their testimony helped convince the jury of Wodke's guilt. Wodke faced the death penalty. During the trial's penalty phase, Wodke took the stand and admitted he'd robbed the Family Mart. But he denied being the shooter. The *Columbia Record* said he testified that he pulled up to the sheriff's cruiser "fixing to stop the car and get out," but "the next thing I saw was a ball of fire" just in front of his chest. He realized Corvette had fired on the officers.

Solicitor Joe Watson pushed Wodke on why he didn't get out and surrender, if that's really what he intended.

Wodke, with his relaxed assuredness, said, "If I'd stopped that car and got out then, I'd have looked like Swiss cheese, buddy, come on."

Gervais Street Bridge looking toward downtown Columbia, near the restaurant where Wodke was captured. *Courtesy of Brandon Dolley via Flickr.*

The jury convicted Wodke of first-degree murder but opted for a life sentence plus twenty-five years rather than death. Rusty Corvette ended up serving eleven years, but after his release, he continued what had been his unsuccessful criminal pattern: commit a crime (robbery or drug smuggling), cut a deal to reduce his time, get out of prison and commit another crime. In 1997, three months after his latest release, he and an accomplice shattered the patio door at an elderly couple's home near Charleston. Their daughter heard the break-in during a phone conversation with her mother and alerted police, who were waiting when the men left the house. Corvette was shot and killed after running into the woods and exchanging gunfire with police.

An armed robbery—no matter how frightening for the victims—wouldn't have earned Sam Wodke a place on a national television show, but his escape from Kirkland Correctional Institution in Columbia and his time on the run did. He'd made other attempts to escape but finally, on January 8, 1994—almost ten years after the robbery and murder—inmate Danny Lail and forty-eight-year-old Sam Wodke drove away from Kirkland in a prison truck. While working on the prison landscape crew, they used a makeshift tool to lift a manhole cover and then crawled through the underground steam tunnels. They had eight hours before the next headcount to cut their way through thick metal mesh gates and a door, subdue some inmates working in the boiler room and steal the keys for a truck. They reportedly did it with only fifteen minutes to spare.

Lail, who had been serving time for two Columbia murders, was soon arrested in Florida.

Wodke, though, remained at large. On March 22, 1996, a segment aired on *Unsolved Mysteries*. Of the many tips received by the call center, the second tip investigated sounded credible. A Colorado woman said a shipyard welder she worked with in Louisiana looked like Wodke. Investigators began tracing the man. Remarkably, Wodke had done nothing to change his appearance. On March 30, officers arrested him at his Louisiana rooming house and returned him to Columbia. He received added time for the escape, and, in August 2005, he died of a heart attack in prison at age sixty.

COLUMBIA'S CAT BURGLAR

For five years, starting in 1974, dozens of homes in Columbia's upscale residential areas, particularly in Forest Acres, were the target of a cat burglar. Once he was unmasked, Richland County sheriff Frank Powell called him a "modern day Jekyll and Hyde." In the years before that unmasking, the cat burglar told others the police were "fumbling fools." As Forest Acres police chief J.C. Rowe said, though, "The police can make a bunch of mistakes. The crook can only make one."

Dressed in dark clothes and gloves, the cat burglar broke in only when no one was home. No one was ever physically harmed. He knew to clip the phone lines to disable alarm systems. He loaded the homeowner's pillowcases with jewelry, gold, silver, coins, valuable firearms and, in one instance, a leopard skin—whatever was easily transportable.

Investigators from Columbia, Forest Acres and the South Carolina Highway Department tracked the break-ins, waiting for that one mistake. That mistake came when the burglar cashed a check for twenty dollars; he'd ripped the blank check from the middle of a checkbook during one of the burglaries. The forged signature and a fake driver's license number written on the check led investigators to Ian Gale.

The burglar's identity shocked the medical and legal communities. Dr. Ian (EYE-an) Gale, a licensed, practicing psychiatrist with a law degree, was well known in Columbia. After his arrest, he became even better known.

Dr. Gale first came to Columbia by way of Pennsylvania, Arizona and Utah, during his two-year stint as an army psychiatrist at Fort Jackson.

He opened his own practice in 1971. While working as a psychiatrist, he attended and graduated from the University of South Carolina School of Law in 1977, where he later taught a popular elective in psychiatry and the law.

Was his life of crime prompted, as claimed, by his growing disillusionment over the nation's economic upheavals in the 1970s, by white supremacist views, by a desire for thrills or to show he was smarter than everyone else? Whatever his reasons, his crime spree began in 1974. He carefully scouted homes, and though he denied he used confidential information from his patients, the word around Columbia was that he sent his patients on "rest cure" trips and burgled their houses while they were gone—and he maybe gave his lawyer and doctor friends wedding gifts of questionable provenance.

Thrills and one-upmanship also played a role for Gale. He obtained several bogus driver's licenses and testified he did it "just to see if it could be done, because it struck his fancy at the time." He admitted to breaking into an insurance company office next door to his psychiatric practice and into the home of an alarm company owner, just for the excitement.

Gale was arrested in July 1979. Police cruisers surrounded his car as he arrived home from his office. Richland County solicitor James Anders said, "We knew he had a weapon with him" and he intended to defend himself, so they were taking no chances.

After his arrest, Dr. Gale helped police clear more than one hundred break-ins, riding around Columbia with officers, pointing out places he'd burgled.

In his home, investigators discovered a nine-by-twelve-foot room he kept sealed from his family. Inside, they found much of his loot, with estimates ranging between $300,000 and $500,000 in value. He also reportedly kept Swiss bank accounts.

He pleaded guilty to eight counts of housebreaking and larceny, receiving a fifteen-year sentence. He wanted to continue to practice medicine while in prison, under the supervision of another physician, but the state medical board permanently revoked his license in 1980. He challenged the revocation, claiming the board's statement that his criminal behavior indicated "sociopathic and possibly psychopathic behavior" had no foundation, but the state Court of Appeals found the South Carolina Board of Medical Examiners acted within its discretion.

He served six years of his sentence and, when released, worked as a security consultant, taught at the community college and, in 1987, published a book on immigrating to Australia. In 1988, he made news again, this time with his announcement he might run for Lexington County sheriff against longtime incumbent Sheriff James Metts. "It's instant name recognition that other people looking for a job don't have," he told reporters. He acknowledged his past raised questions about his integrity, but as a born-again Christian, he felt the changes he'd made in his life would speak for themselves. Metts was reelected.

Rather than head to Australia, though, he moved to Swansea, just south of Columbia, where he and his wife of twenty years lived on twelve acres in a house heated by a wood stove and with no air-conditioning. For one of the most colorful characters in Columbia's crime history, a man whose acquaintances acknowledged him as brilliant, he lived a simple life. His wife died in August 2017. A little more than a month later, he set his house on fire and shot himself in the head. He was seventy-nine years old.

ALIMONY AND MURDER

One Lexington County divorce raised an unusual question: Can a woman who tried to have her husband killed collect alimony in the divorce? Murder-for-hire in a divorce case is not unique, as it turned out, but is certainly unusual.

Dorothy Sharpe sued her husband, Russell Larry Sharpe, for divorce in 1986. A Lexington County judge granted the divorce and ordered the husband to maintain his ex-wife's health insurance on his business account as alimony. In addition to the health coverage as alimony, the wife was awarded 35 percent of the marital estate and attorney fees.

Husband and wife appealed the decision, complaining that the judge didn't consider the physical cruelty during the marriage and that the estate wasn't divided fairly. At the end of the list of complaints was the husband's contention he shouldn't have to pay for her health insurance. However, she was suffering from terminal cancer and would likely be unable to get insurance elsewhere, so the appeals court upheld the award—even though she had confessed that she'd conspired to kill him.

One judge thought the issue of getting alimony even after confessing to an attempted murder needed more explanation. Surprisingly, the situation was not without precedent, and the court's opinion dispassionately dissected similar cases from other states. The wife argued that her one attempt at conspiring to murder happened after they separated, wasn't what caused the divorce, didn't reduce the marital assets and didn't actually hurt anybody.

She argued it wasn't fair that her one moment of poor judgment should "trigger a windfall to the husband," especially since he'd also misbehaved by committing adultery and by mistreating her during their marriage.

In the divorce proceeding and on appeal, judges took the case on its facts—and argued all such cases should be considered on an individual basis. In other words, no hard rule exists in South Carolina that a wife who wishes her husband dead and takes some steps to make that happen will be automatically barred from alimony.

REFERENCES

1. THE NEW FORENSICS

Suicide or Murder?

Bovsun, Mara. "Poisoned Packages: Using the Mail for Murder." *New York Daily News*, February 20, 2011.

Keowee Courier. "Hayes Pardoned: Testimony of Handwriting Experts—General Review of the Case." July 4, 1906.

———. "Hayes Sentence Commuted: Carvalho, Handwriting Expert." October 19, 1904.

Moss, Jennifer, Assistant Curator, Oconee History Museum. Hoyt Hayes research file, accessed July 2022.

National Research Council. *Strengthening Forensic Science in the United States: A Path Forward.* Washington, D.C.: National Academies Press, 2009. http://nap.edu/12589.

State v. Hayes, 48 S.E. 251 (June 1904).

The Sumter Does

Breeding, Brittany. "The Lives of Pamela Buckley and James Freund, Sumter County's 1976 Jane and John Doe." *WACH Fox 57* (Columbia, SC), January 22, 2021. https://wach.com.

Collins, Jeffrey. "Lancaster Man Identified 44 Years after Being Found Dead in South Carolina; Cold Case Reopened." *Lancaster (PA) Online*, January 22, 2021. https://lancasteronline.com.

Daily Times-News (Burlington, NC). "Bodies Remain Unidentified." September 19, 1976.

DNA Doe Project. "Sumter Jane Doe 1976: Success Stories." https://dnadoeproject.org.

The Doe Network. "189UFSC—Unidentified Female" (Sumter female Doe). https://www.doenetwork.org.

———. "198UMSC—Unidentified Male" (Sumter male Doe). https://www.doenetwork.org.

McDaniel, Matthew. Sumter Mystery Couple. https://sumtermysterycouple.com.

Neaves, Alicia. "Upstate Man Credited with Helping Identify John and Jane Doe in Sumter County." *WLTX News 19*, January 21, 2021. https://www.wltx.com.

California Cop Killer

Broder, John M. "After 45 Years, an Arrest in the Killing of 2 Officers." *New York Times*, January 30, 2003. https://www.nytimes.com.

"Columbia Man Accused of 1957 Murders Enters Guilty Pleas." *WIS TV News 10*, March 24, 2003. https://www.wistv.com.

Harnisch, Larry. "Death in El Segundo." *LA Daily Mirror*, July 22, 2011. https://ladailymirror.com.

Hoover, Marc. "Officers Down: Six Bullets for Two Police Officers." *Clermont (OH) Sun*, July 12 and July 19, 2019. https://www.clermontsun.com.

Leung, Rebecca. "Cold-Blooded Crime Haunts Investigators for Half a Century." *CBS News 48 Hours*, October 1, 2004. https://www.cbsnews.com.

"Marked for Life." *Forensic Files*, Season 10, Episode 1, May 18, 2005.

2. THE MISSING (AND FOUND)

The Shaw Creek Killer

Blundell, R.H., and G. Haswell Wilson. *Trial of Buck Ruxton*. London: William Hodge & Co., 1937, 1950.

The Doe Network. 46UFSC—Unidentified Female. Aiken Doe, January 25, 1993. https://www.doenetwork.org.

———. 7UFSC—Unidentified Female. Aiken Doe, November 16, 1987. https://www.doenetwork.org.

Johnson, Bianca Cain. "Woman's Slaying in 1992 Tought to Be by Serial Killer." *Augusta Chronicle*, August 21, 2016. https://www.augustachronicle.com.

National Institutes of Health. "Visible Proofs: The Buck Ruxton 'Jigsaw Murders' Case." https://www.nlm.nih.gov.

Oxygen True Crime. "The Disappearance of the Millbrook Twins: Missing Twin Sisters Case Still Unsolved." November 23, 2019. https://www.oxygen.com.

Time. "Great Britain: Dreadful and Gruesome." March 23, 1936. https://time.com

Whelan, Micheal. "The Shaw Creek Killer." *Unresolved* podcast. https://unresolved.me.

Snatched from Her Bed

DiBiase, Tad. Table of No Body Cases. https://www.nobodycases.com.

"Mother Wonders when 'Closer' Means 'Closed' in 21-Year-Old Case." *WIS TV News 10*, January 11, 2008; updated January 15, 2008. https://www.wistv.com.

Robinson, Hannah, and Sophie Keyes Hoge. "Bond Denied for Suspect in Guttierez [*sic*] Case." *WIS TV News 10*. January 6, 2022; updated January 14, 2022. https://www.wistv.com.

"Solicitor Responds to Accusations of Holding Up 21-Year-Old Case." WIS TV News 10, November 29, 2007; updated December 3, 2007. https://www.wistv.com.

The Survivor Who Thrived

Escaping Captivity: The Kara Robinson Story. Oxygen, first aired September 26, 2021.

Fanning, Diane. *Into the Water*. New York: St. Martin's, 2004.

Tempesta, Erica. "Woman Who Escaped a Serial Killer After He Kidnapped Her as a Teen Shares Her Traumatic Story on TikTok." *Daily Mail*, September 22, 2020. https://www.dailymail.co.uk.

3. THE LADY KILLERS

Beatrice Snipes

Dorn, T. Felder, with Jean A. Ghent. *Death of a Policeman, Birth of a Baby*. N.p., 2012.

Reynolds, Ruth. "A Little Child Leads Mother." *Daily News* (New York), March 25, 1945.

The State. "Mrs. Snipes Bewildered at Fate Engulfing Her." December 12, 1932.

Wincka, Mark. "Jean Ghent Saved Her Mother from the Electric Chair." *Salisbury Post*, November 28, 2012. https://www.salisburypost.com.

Rose Stinnette

Florence Morning News. "Four Held Here on Murder Charge, Inquest Tonight." April 30, 1946.

———. "Justice Moves Swiftly in Sessions Court." June 25, 1946.

———. "Seen About Town." June 21, 1946.

Greenville (SC) *News*. "Negress Slated to Be Executed." January 17, 1947.

Lyon, Edward, and David Reutter. "South Carolina Judge Halts State Executions by Electrocution and Firing Squad." *Prison Legal News*, November 2022, 20. https://www.prisonlegalnews.org.

Pittsburgh Courier. "Sparks Fly, Electrocute Dixie Woman." *February 1, 1947*.

Sigmon v. Stirling and SC Dept. of Corrections. Complaint for Temporary, Preliminary, and Injunctive Relief and Declaratory Judgment, U.S. Federal District Court of South Carolina, filed June 3, 2021.

Spokesman-Review (Spokane, WA). "Smiling Negro Woman Meets End Cheerfully." January 18, 1947.

Jennie May Walker Burleson

Burleson v. Burleson, 126 S.W.2d 676 (1939).

Dorn, T. Felder. *The Downfall of Galveston's May Walker Burleson*. Charleston, SC: The History Press, 2018. An impeccably researched and readable account of the case and its backdrop.

New York Times. "Test for Mrs. Burleson; Slayer of Successor as Wife Put in Mental Hospital." March 16, 1940.

4. The Poisoners

A Short History of Poison

Aiken Standard. "Sentences." September 26, 1917.
State v. Glover, 4 S.E. 564 (1888) (attempted asafetida poisoning).
State v. Ready, 96 S.E. 287 (S.C. 1918) (poisoned well).

Lieutenant Samuel Epes

Barnett, Joe. "Wife-Slayer Epes Is Granted Parole: Victim's Parents Protest." *The State*, December 4, 1959.
McKinney, James. "Epes Loses Clemency Plea." *Columbia Record*, November 25, 1946.
State v. Epes, 39 S.E.2d 769 (1946) (Seconal).

A Modern Arsenic Poisoning

Bender, Chris. "Bond Set in Arsenic Case; Neighbors, Family Testify in Court." *Beaufort Gazette*, April 16, 2002.
Crites, Ben. "Delays in Trials May Last for Years." *Island Packet* (Hilton Head, SC), June 4, 2006.
Greenville News. "Millionaire's Wife Charged in Husband's Death." April 13, 2002.
Monk, John. "Millionaire's Arsenic Death still a Mystery." *The State*, March 10, 2002.
———. "Rich Wife Could Be Tried This Year in Arsenic Death." *The State*, February 13, 2005.
"Newberry Woman Accused of Poisoning Husband Arraigned Friday." *WIS TV News 10*, April 12, 2002; updated February 27, 2003. https://www.wistv.com.
Obituary, Alfred Spotts. *Greenville News*, August 8, 2001.
The State. "Wife Freed on Bail in Poisoning Death." April 17, 2002.
Times and Democrat (Orangeburg, SC). "Arsenic Death of Newberry Millionaire Leaves Accusations." March 11, 2002.

5. Headline Crimes

Pee Wee Gaskins

Beaty, Jim. *Pee Wee and Me.* https://issuu.com/thebrandinggarden/docs/pee_wee_and_me_final_manuscript_mar.
[Note: The few pages of the manuscript completed were uploaded by Dr. Beatty's daughter, Elizabeth Hall, on March 7, 2018. His book was also a resource for the 2021 podcast, Pee Wee Gaskins Was Not My Friend, hosted by Jeff Keating. See https://www.facebook.com/doghousepictures1/.]
Gaskins, Donald "Pee Wee," with Wilton Earle. *Final Truth.* New York: Pinnacle, 1993.
Harris, Art. "The Seeds of Vengeance." *Washington Post*, June 24, 1983. https://www.washingtonpost.com.
Query, Grady. *Pee Wee*, vols. 1 and 2. N.p.: AuthorHouse, 2014.
State v. Gaskins, 326 S.E.2d 132 (1984).

Home Alone

Companion Property Ins. v. Airborne Express, 631 S.E.2d 915 (S.C. App. 2006).
Enfinger, Matthew. "Murder and Life of Jessica Lynne Carpenter Still Remembered after 20 Years." *Aiken Standard*, August 8, 2020; updated April 13, 2021. https://www.postandcourier.com.
Martin, Sandi. "Man Admits Guilt in Death." *Augusta Chronicle*, May 18, 2006. https://www.augustachronicle.com.
Rivera v. State, 647 S.E.2d 70 (Ga. 2007).

A Terrifying Summer

Bell v. Evatt, 72 F.3d 421 (1995).
Bovsun, Mara. "South Carolina Serial Killer Forced Girl to Write a Farewell Note and Tormented His Victims' Families After Sick Spree in Mid-80s." *New York Daily News*, November 15, 2014. https://www.nydailynews.com.
Douglas, John, and Mark Olshaker. *When a Killer Calls.* New York: William Morrow, 2022.

Frankie, C.M. "Ret. FBI Profiler John Douglas on Larry Gene Bell, 'One of the Most Sadistic Murderers He's Investigated.'" *A&E TV True Crime Blog*, January 26, 2022. https://www.aetv.com.

Shuler, Rita. *Murder in the Midlands: Larry Gene Bell and the 28 Days of Terror That Shook South Carolina*. Charleston, SC: The History Press, 2007.

State v. Bell, 393 S.E.2d 364 (1988).

6. The Gamblers

"I'm Going to Disney World!"

Firestone, David. "South Carolina High Court Derails Video Poker Games." *New York Times*, October 15, 1999. https://www.nytimes.com.

Fox, Stan. "South Carolina Gambling Laws." LetsGambleUSA, December 7, 2022. https://www.letsgambleusa.com.

Hess v. Medlock, 820 F.2d 1368 (4th Cir. 1987).

Kuenzie, Jack. "30 Years Ago, A Day I Will Never Forget." *WIS TV News*, January 28, 2016. https://www.wistv.com.

Levenson, Bob, and Jim Leusner. "Death Hoax Unravels at Epcot; Tourists Recognize Ex-Police Chief, Friend on the Run." *Orlando Sentinel*, January 28, 1986. https://www.orlandosentinel.com.

New York Times. "Ex-Police Chief Offers an Apology for Scandal." July 13, 1986. https://www.nytimes.com.

O'Brien, John. "Did Police Chief Get Carried Away by Love or Death?" *Chicago Tribune*, September 10, 1985. https://www.chicagotribune.com.

Scoppe, Rick. "Police Chief Given Suspended Sentence." *APNews*, July 10, 1986. https://apnews.com.

Gambling Debts and Death

Beeker, LaDonna. "No Prison Time for Columbia Men in Sports Betting Operation." *WIS News 10*, March 24, 2016. https://www.wistv.com.

Monk, John. "Federal Jury Finds 2 SC Men Guilty of Operating Gambling Ring." *Charlotte Observer*, January 27, 2016. https://www.charlotteobserver.com.

"The Mystery at Ascot Estates." *Dateline NBC*, February 18, 2021.

Phillips, Noelle. "Brett Parker Trial Fallout: The Anatomy of a Sports Betting Operation." Off Shore Gaming Association, June 17, 2013. https://osga.com.

State v. Parker. Unpublished Opinion No. 2015-UP-001238. (S.C. App. 2015).

U.S. v. Parker, 790 F.3d 550 (4th Cir. 2015).

7. The Tricksters

Terror Close to Home

Adcox, Seanna. "Rita Bixby, Guilty in Killings of 2 Officers After Leaving N.H." Boston.com, September 14, 2011. http://archive.boston.com.

Anti-Defamation League. *The Lawless Ones: The Resurgence of the Sovereign Citizen Movement*, 2nd ed. https://www.adl.org.

FBI Counterterrorism Analysis Section. "Sovereign Citizens: A Growing Domestic Threat to Law Enforcement." *Law Enforcement Bulletin*, September 1, 2011. https://leb.fbi.gov.

Johnson, Daryl. "Sovereign Citizen Wanted for Fatal Shooting Finally Apprehended in Florida." Southern Poverty Law Center, August 29, 2018. https://www.splcenter.org.

Moser, Bob. "'Patriot' Shootout in Abbeville, S.C. Raises Questions About the Town's Extremist Past." Southern Poverty Law Center, April 20, 2004. https://www.splcenter.org.

Robins, Kayla. "Sheriff: Sumter Auto Shop Shooting Suspect Is Sovereign Citizen." *The Item* (Sumter), August 13, 2018.

Sarteschi, Christine M. "Sovereign Citizens: A Narrative Review of Implications of Violence Toward Law Enforcement." *Aggression and Violent Behavior*, September–October 2021. 10.1016/j.avb.2020.101509.

State v. Rita Bixby. 644 S.E.2d 54 (2007).

State v. Rita Bixby. S.C. App. Ct. Opinion No. 4768, December 17, 2010. Note: After her death, the court withdrew this opinion and agreed to abate the appeal, but didn't abate it *ab initio*, which would have returned her to the status she had before she was initially charged. *State v. Bixby*, 723 S.E.2d 841 (2011).

State v. Steven Bixby. 698 S.E.2d 572 (2010).

Insurance Fraud

Carroll, Mike J. *Irish Travellers: An Undocumented Journey Through History*. N.p., 2018.

Lind, J.R. "Love and Death Among the Irish Travellers." *Nashville Scene*, April 29, 2021. https://www.nashvillescene.com.

Monk, John. "25 More Irish Travelers Plan to Plead Guilty to Fraud Charges." *The State*, August 23, 2017.

Reardon, Patrick T. "The Highway Is Their Home." *Chicago Tribune*, March 17, 2000. https://www.chicagotribune.com..

Tampa Bay Times. "Disney Rape Claim Called a Scam." October 7, 1993; updated October 10, 2005. https://www.tampabay.com.

Wright, Don. *Scam! Inside America's Con Artist Clans*. Elkhart, IN: Cottage Publications, 1996.

The Minister and the Hitman

Columbia Record. "Leroy Jenkins Now Free Man." February 18, 1988.

Galloway, Jim, and Rick Ricks. "Who Is Rev. LeRoy Jenkins?" *Anderson Independent*, April 8, 1979, 1. Start of three-part series.

Ghose, Dave. "From the Archives: Leroy Jenkins Starts Over.: *Columbus Monthly*, June 22, 2017. https://www.columbusmonthly.com.

Kapsidelis, Tom. "Jenkins Dealt Stunning Blow in City He Claims to Love." *The State*, May 23, 1979.

Mansfield, Duncan. "Faith Healer Jenkins Arrested." *Greenville News*, April 18, 1979.

Fire at the Farm

Anderson (Trustee for Estate of Billy E. Graham) v. Citizens Bank, et al. 365 S.E.2d 26 (S.C. App. 1987).

Associated Press. "Judge Keeps Doors Shut on Olanta Murder Trial." *The State*, May 8, 1991.

Fritz, John. "When Friendship Ends." *The Item* (Sumter, SC), May 14, 1989.

The Item (Sumter, SC). "2 in Graham Murder Case Granted New Trials." May 16, 1991.

State v. McCray. 506 S.E.2d 301 (1998).

State v. Prince. 447 S.E.2d 177 (1993).

State v. Smith. 477 S.E.2d 175 (1993).

8. Political Scandals

Lost Trust

Brack, Andy. "Operation Lost Trust: Twenty Years Later." *Post & Courier* (Charleston, SC), July 14, 2010; updated May 16, 2019. https://www.postandcourier.com.

Crangle, John. *Operation Lost Trust and the Ethics Reform Movement*. N.p.: Crangle Co., 2015.

Greer, Ben. *Presumed Guilty: The Tim Wilkes Story*. Charleston, SC: Wyrick & Co., 1995.

Pierce, Jon B. "Operation Lost Trust, 1989–1999." *South Carolina Encyclopedia*. https://www.scencyclopedia.org.

Scoppe, Cindi Ross. "Federal Judge Stings Lost Trust; 5 Cases Dismissed as Court Cries 'Fraud.'" *The State*, March 1, 1997

Abscam

Cascone, Sarah. "An Evicted Princess Is Refusing to Vacate a Roman Villa That's Home to Caravaggio's Only Ceiling Mural." *Artnet*, January 23, 2023. https://news.artnet.com.

Clark, John F., and Cookie Miller VanSice. *Capitol Steps and Missteps: The Wild, Improbable Ride of Congressman John Jenrette*. N.P.: CreateSpace, 2017.

Jacobson v. U.S. 503 U.S. 540 (1992).

Jenrette, Rita, with Kathleen Maxa. "The Liberation of a Congressional Wife." *Playboy*, April 1981.

Levy, Ariel. "Letter from Rome: The Renovation." *New Yorker*, November 28, 2011.

Mathews v. U.S. 485 U.S. 58 (1988).

The Reliable Source. "Rita Jenrette's New Take On an Old Sex Scandal: That Night on the Capitol Steps." *Washington Post*, November 28, 2011. https://web.archive.org.

So, Jimmy. "The Real Story and Lesson of the Abscam Sting in 'American Hustle.'" *Daily Beast*, December 17, 2013; updated July 11, 2017. https://www.thedailybeast.com.

9. The Legislative Daughters

Did He? Or Didn't He?

Brown v. Mississippi. 297 U.S. 278 (1936).

"Carrie Baker LeNoir: Breaking Down Barriers." South Carolina Firefighters Association, March 1, 2022. https://scfirefighters.org.

Frazier v. Cupp, 394 U.S. 731 (1969).

Hunter, Brad. "Crime Hunter: Serial Killer Junior Pierce a Loser in Life and Death." *Toronto Sun*, August 8, 2020. https://torontosun.com.

LeNoir, Carrie Baker. *Beyond Reasonable Doubt*. Horatio, SC: P&R Enterprises, 1992.

McGraw, Seamus. "Outrage: The Peg Cuttino Story." CrimeLibrary.com, reprinted as "William Pierce Jr." Murderpedia. https://murderpedia.org/male.P/p/pierce-william.htm.

Simon, Stephanie. "Getting Suspects to Confess." *Los Angeles Times*, September 21, 1995. https://www.latimes.com.

State v. Pierce. 207 S.E.2d 414 (1974).

A Family Divided

Feeley, Jef. "They Call Him 'Mr. Murder.'" *National Law Journal*, May 25, 1987.

LeBlanc, Clif, and Wendy Warren. "Beckham Gets Life, Families Say Decision Will Help Start Healing." *The State*, October 5, 1996.

Monk, John. "'Mr. Murder' Looms Large in S.C. Courts; Flamboyant Lawyer Defends Suspects That Others Shun." *Charlotte Observer*, April 16, 1989.

Moorefield, April E. "Aunt: Beckham Asked Wife to Visit Alone." *Greenville News*, September 25, 1996.

———. "Ex-Bouncer Lays Out Grisly Details of Beckham Murder Plot." *Greenville News*, September 22, 1996.

"Newberry: Small Town Justice." *City Confidential*, Season 2, episode 12. Aired January 17, 2000.

Pilkington, Ed. "The Business of Securing Death Sentences: 40 Years and 28 Men." *Guardian*, May 5, 2017. https://www.theguardian.com.

State v. Beckham. 513 S.E.2d 606 (1999).

10. SIDE TRIPS, CRIME BITS AND ODDITIES

Vicious Politics

Monk, John. "Bitter S.C. Feud Led to 1903 'Crime of the Century.'" *The State*, January 12, 2003.

Professor Greener

Berry, Rebecca Rego. "Reclaiming Abandoned African Americana." In *Rare Books Uncovered: True Stories of Fantastic Finds in Unlikely Places*, 196–200. Minneapolis: Voyageur Press, 2005.

Cop Killer, Escapee and TV Fugitive

Bryant, Bobby. "Suspect in Slaying Arrested." *The State*, November 30, 1985.

Columbia Record. "Wodke Found Guilty in Patrolman's Death." March 8, 1986.

Gilmer, Bryan. "Charleston Police Kill Man Involved in '85 Slaying of Greenville Constable." *Greenville News*, February 7, 1997.

Greenville News. "Crime Show to Film Segment on Wodke." February 17, 1994.

Simmons, Chris. "Traces of Terror Linger for Victims of Holiday Siege." *Greenville News*, November 27, 1986.

Columbia's Cat Burglar

Bryan (Ohio) Times. "Ex-Cat Burglar Wants to Be Sheriff." March 24, 1988.

Daily News (Bowling Green, KY). "Psychiatrist by Day, Cat Burglar by Night?" July 27, 1979.

Gale, Ian. *Successful Migrating to Australia*. London: Queen Anne Press, 1990; Australia: Migrant Information Press, 1987.

Gale v. State Board of Med. Exam. of SC. 320 S.E.2d 35 (1984).

LeBlanc, Clif. "Doctor Who Burglarized More than 100 Homes in Columbia Area Kills Himself." *The State*, October 3, 2017. https://www.thestate.com.

Alimony and Murder

Sharpe v. Sharpe. 416 S.E.2d 215 (1992).

ABOUT THE AUTHOR

Cathy Pickens, a lawyer and college professor, is a crime fiction writer (*Southern Fried Mysteries*, St. Martin's/Minotaur; re-released as *Blue Ridge Mountain Mysteries* by Joffe Books) and true crime columnist for *Mystery Readers Journal*. She taught law in the McColl School of Business and served as provost at Queens, as national president of Sisters in Crime and on the boards of Mystery Writers of America and the Mecklenburg Forensic Medicine Program (an evidence collection/preservation training collaborative). She is also the author of *CREATE!* (ICSC Press), offers coaching and workshops on developing the creative process and works with writers on telling their stories.

Other books from Cathy Pickens and The History Press include:

Charleston Mysteries
Charlotte True Crime Stories
Triangle True Crime Stories
True Crime Stories of Eastern North Carolina
True Crime Stories of Upstate South Carolina
True Crime Stories of Western North Carolina

Visit us at
www.historypress.com